GOYA

Goya

BY

CHARLES POORE

CHARLES SCRIBNER'S SONS · NEW YORK
CHARLES SCRIBNER'S SONS · LTD · LONDON
1938

FOR MARY

"Decíamos ayer . . ."
—FRAY LUIS DE LEÓN

Contents

Illustrations

I
Goya

I

Goya

FRANCISCO JOSÉ GOYA Y LUCIENTES was born at Fuendetodos, in Aragon, March 30, 1746. He died on the sixteenth
of April, 1828, in exile at Bordeaux.

HIS expression was singularly lacking in humility. In all the
portraits of himself there is a glance of stubborn arrogance:
the eyes are deep in the skull, the chin is truculent, the nose
is broader than one would suppose from a profile. It is apparent that he was not as tall as he would like to be; the
others around him loom over him, though he stretches a full
five feet seven or eight. Yet there was a force in him that
outlasted them. He was there to bury most of his friends
and to send some of his enemies to hell before their time.

He had a chest like a sherry cask. The ravages of time and
injudicious pleasures spared him longer than they usually
spare far more prudent men. Illness hounded him at intervals. Yet he was powerful enough to survive more than eight
decades of uncommonly strenuous life, agile enough to have
been an amateur bullfighter, hardy enough to cross the
Pyrenees alone on a mule at eighty and lusty enough to make
plausible the tales of many wenching escapades and the
twenty legitimate children.

[3]

A racy and sardonic humor carried him through a notorious court. He satirized it unmercifully. He was painter to the king in a flagrant time. He saw Spain smashed under the gun-butts of an Italian-born invader. He lived in an epoch of revolution and reaction, and he dramatized the crucial confrontations that still shake civilization.

He had more genius and more faults than most men. He liked hunting and the bullring and he was appalled by the cruelties he saw in madhouses, in prisons and in the dunce-capped pageantry of the Inquisition. He enjoyed singing and drinking and playing the guitar.

All Spain is in the enormous range and volume of his work. In that great mountain square between Europe and Africa there has never been another man who so completely saw every aspect of that world. Here are the pretty, distracting duchesses and here are the people dead of the hunger, guns and pestilence Napoleon brought to Spain. Here is the twisted zeal of the Inquisition and here is the hag-ridden mythology of the peninsula, here are the hunters in the field, the smugglers in the mountains, the beggars in the streets, the festivals of Madrid, the heroism of the *Dos de Mayo*, the spectacles of the bullring, the peasants and the grandees of Spain. All Spain. And Goya had the grasp and the understanding and the skill to give it a furious, timeless eloquence.

For in the vast gallery of Goya's work, from the stiff, convention-bound paintings of the early days, through the airs and graces of the middle years when he verged upon the Gainsboroughesque, to the free and magnificent impressionism of his last and greatest time, an epoch is reflected through its personalities. To know who these men and women were is to know what Spain was in the age of Goya. He rarely drew or painted anything without human figures in it; he was little interested in landscapes or still life; he could never find people enough. Sanchez Cantón observed that perhaps the most accurate description of Goya is "painter of humanity," and no one will deny the felicity of the expression.

3

GOYA towered over the painters of his own day, truly enough; yet that is an inadequate measure of his ability, for the Spanish painters of his time were contentedly mediocre. And it is important to remember that he was a part of the Spanish tradition in art, not, as many have supposed, an isolated figure. For, as Beruete has said, this man, who seems "so individual and apart, who was born in a hidden corner of the land of Aragon, and who at first sight appears as an isolated and solitary genius, independent, without tradition and without school, is not this if we look closer, but, notwithstanding his originality and his varied outlook, is quite the contrary; he is a Spaniard to the very marrow and a man of his time as well as his race."

That is well said. Though there is perhaps more than a shade of nationalistic wish-fulfillment in Beruete's laboring of the point when he goes on to say that Goya's "task is in fact the continuation of Spanish painting, of that painting of the sixteenth and seventeenth centuries which had been forgotten and superseded by foreign influences in the years preceding those in which he lived. His it is to be the link which was to unite that which was to come with that which had been, determining, at the same time as his own period of transition, those principles of the graphic arts which could form part of the progress of our painting; and hence, as an ultimate result of Spanish creation, of even those elements which later came to influence universal art outside our nation, originating in this way one of the most important phases of what is now called modern art."[1]

Goya's place in Spain's art is secure enough to make the customary comparison with Greco and Velasquez a matter of partisanship rather than merit. Indeed, it has been reduced to a mathematical proposition by Madariaga, who once suggested to Sanchez Cantón that he ranked them in this way:

Invention: Goya first, Greco second, Velasquez third.
Emotion: Greco first, Goya second, Velasquez third.
Technique: Velasquez first, Goya second, Greco third.

It is an ingenious enough scheme; only the very solemn would bother seriously to question the ranking or even to suggest that the arbitrary choice of qualities itself invalidates any pretence the judgment might have to ultimate finality. In a solemn mood, then, I should say that the only thing wrong with the Madariaga parallels is that Goya should obviously be first in the second and third categories as well as in the quality of invention. Advocates of Greco or Velasquez should certainly suggest the same objective sort of rearrangement for those two artists.

4

THE political commentary in Goya's art has neither weakened it as art, nor has it wholly lost its application to later

[1]*Goya As Portrait Painter*. By A. de Beruete y Moret. Translated by Selwyn Brinton. Houghton Mifflin. 1922.

THE COLOSSUS

times. To understand Goya it is helpful to know something about the history of his time, certainly; but to see the works of Goya is to understand more about that time than many pages of history may supply.

The astute Hume, for example, has said that Spain in the last half of the eighteenth century and early in the nineteenth—which was precisely Goya's time—"presented the curious phenomenon of a nation in which the great mass of the people lagged far behind successive governments in their desire for progress and reform."[1] Yet it was not willingly that they remained mediæval.

If it is true, as Hume says, that "the quickening of thought, the emancipation of expression, the philosophical theories which preceded the great uprising of the French Revolution had stopped at the barrier of the Pyrenees," and that "with the exception of a comparatively few travelled and enlightened men who were looked upon by their compatriots as dangerous innovators, Voltaireans and Freemasons," the people of Spain "demanded nothing better than to live in their own way in peace, giving blind love and obedience to their kings, and equally blind compliance with the forms of their faith, which in the great majority of cases had degenerated to the grossest and blackest superstition," we have only to look at Goya's unforgettable drawings to see that the people were far from happy under that state of affairs.

Goya lived, as we do, in the tumult of a pre-war, war, and post-war time. The unending series of alliances that led to wars and the wars that led to new alliances were as much

[1]*Modern Spain: 1788–1898.* By Martin Hume. G. P. Putnam's Sons. 1900.

a part of the theoretically enlightened policy of the Neapolitan Charles III as of the demonstrably blundering policy of his Neapolitan-born son, Charles IV.

War with England was not rare in Goya's youth; openly or covertly the world-wide struggle of these two imperial powers with inimical ambitions went on. Charles III was at war with England in the seventeen sixties; he was always hopeful—what Spanish government has not been?—of seeing Spain's flag again at Gibraltar. He did not succeed, and neither did his maladroit son, though by that time the struggle against England was changing toward the ultimate alliance with her against Napoleon. Before that came about, however, there were various attempts on the part of Spain's rulers to fight successfully on the side of the French.

5

IT was a world strewn with treasons and disasters, where only plunderers were triumphant and only a satirist could do full justice to the scene.

Goya's years of greatest prosperity came in the disastrous reign of Charles IV, between 1789—that date known for so vastly more important reasons to the world—when he was proclaimed in Madrid, and 1808, when he first gave way before Ferdinand, his son, and then before Napoleon.

It would have been futile to expect any good to come to Spain under so witless a ruler as Charles IV in the most favorable years; it was tragic, in the epoch of Napoleon. Beneficent as the most admiring historians of Charles III may have found that "enlightened despot's" reign, it had not made Spain prosperous. The cost of fighting England for the losing cause of colonial empire had not only been immense but use-less, for when Charles III supported the American colonies against England he gave his own colonies hopes of freedom that they were not many decades in realizing.

Charles IV inherited that debt as well as the lost cause. And when he tried to turn to France for help he found France in the throes of a revolution that was sweeping away the chance of Bourbon solidarity. Indeed, Charles IV tried to save the throne of Louis XVI, and when his efforts to do that failed, he entertained, for a time, a rosy faith in the chance that the French, grown weary of liberty, might invite him—of all people—to take over their throne. Stranger things had been known to happen. But nothing personally fortunate ever happened to Charles IV. He went out—and Napoleon came in.

Goya's *Desastres de la Guerra* show in terms of human lives what those years of battle, famine and destruction—from 1808 to 1814—meant to Spain. For though many of their leaders (some, no doubt, believing honestly that the rule of Napoleon's puppet king, Joseph, was better than the rule of Charles IV, Godoy or Ferdinand) had gone over to the Napoleonic side, become *afrancesados*, the people of Spain fought on.

They knew, after the superb victory of the Spanish forces at Bailen in 1808, after the siege of Zaragoza, above all after the Dos de Mayo in Madrid, that Spain had fire and cour-age enough to oppose Napoleon. A people who would not be beaten could not be beaten by a foreign invader. And they had the help of the British under Wellington, who had been sent into Spain to carry on England's war against Napoleon.

While juntas carried on Spanish rule in spite of the decrees of Joseph, and the *guerilleros* harassed the Napoleonic troops all over the Peninsula, the first great modern charter of Spanish freedom was being written by the representatives of the Spanish people at Cadiz, in 1812.

Mild as the Constitution of Cadiz seems in retrospect, it brought forth the furious antagonism of every feudal element. When Ferdinand returned from Valencay in 1814, after the Napoleonic forces had been beaten he swore to be bound by it. He soon broke his word, and instituted the most barbarous and repressive measures of the old régime. After Riego's rebellion touched off the Revolution of 1820, Ferdinand was forced to rule under the Constitution of 1812. For three years Spain struggled toward a liberal government. But in 1823 a foreign invasion once more restored the rule of reaction, when the Duke of Angoulême invaded Spain to get back for Ferdinand the power to oppress his own people. From then on Ferdinand and his *camarilla* of sadists and buffoons held power in Spain to the end of Goya's life.

But Goya, like many others, preferred exile to life in Spain during that bloodswept time.

6

Too much has been made of his anti-clericalism by the romantic; too much has been made of his manifestations of piety by the zealous. To say that Goya was a very religious man would be to overstate the case. After all, he is famous for some impious art. Yet he is also famous for paintings that were made for the Church, accepted by the Church and praised by the Church. In spite of being at times in the bad graces of the Inquisition he was never cast out. To the end of his days he did religious paintings.

Spain regarded that paradox with an equanimity based on custom. The opinions of worldly clerics his drawings expressed were widely shared. Even in recent times priests might be seen in the Prado smiling over them. And a Carthusian at Zaragoza who showed me Goya's murals for Aula Dei remarked that Goya was a great artist, but that he was perhaps less engrossed in religion than in *las mujeres y los toros* —the women and the bulls.

You may place what interpretation you please on Goya's etching of the men laughing at the monk sorrowing over two money bags, or the drawing of the priest whispering to the woman, or the workman with the priest on his back, or the nun frightened by a cassocked ghost playing a guitar, and yet not reconcile them with the simple piety of his "Christ in the Garden," unless you understand that Goya recorded what he saw, and that what he saw in the Spain of his time was not always wholly bad any more than it was wholly good. He painted and drew what he wanted to paint and draw, too, no doubt. For it never really need come as such a surprise as people sometimes profess that an artist who exposes the follies of others may have follies of his own. Nor does it—since he above all should know—invalidate his commentary.

Goya was baptized at Fuendetodos the day after he was born. His brother was a priest, he signed his letters with the cross, he distinguished, as many Spaniards have always distinguished, between the faith and some of its administrators on earth. His bones, after many wanderings, were buried at last in a church, in San Antonio de la Florida on the banks of Madrid's Manzanares River, under the dome that he himself had decorated with a gallery of angels, laughing spectators and saints drawn from the living gallery of eighteenth-century Madrid.

7

GOYA was not a revolutionist: he was a revolution. He began his career in art as a painter of personages; his immortality rests most securely on his drawings of the people of Spain. His hatred of Ferdinand VII's barbarous oppression is as searingly expressed as his scorn of the court's pomposities. He said that "the dream of reason produces monsters," and he drew the savage and incomparable *Caprichos*, the *Desastres de la Guerra* and the *Disparates*, three records of folly, war and superstition. Yet he also painted some of the most serene portraits of children in all art. His friends were among the advanced men of the time who believed in the ideas of freedom and the rights of man that were sifting across the Pyrenees from France in spite of all the court's efforts to keep them out of a still mediæval land. "If Truth should die, who would mourn her?" he asked in one of the most memorable of the *Disparates*. And the companion plate shows the people who mourned Truth's death terrified and infuriated at her unwelcome resurrection.

Swift's own epitaph—in the lines of Yeats—is remarkably appropriate to Goya. For:

> *Savage indignation there*
> *Cannot lacerate his breast.*
> *Imitate him if you dare,*
> *World-besotted traveler; he*
> *Served human liberty.*

II

Youth and the Legend

[1746–1772]

II

Youth and the Legend
[1746–1772]

I

FUENDETODOS is a stone village that goes in steps up the side of a steep hillside on the scarred Aragonese plain nearly thirty miles by winding road from Zaragoza. Francisco José Goya y Lucientes was born there to José Goya and Gracia Lucientes.

José lived by various and obscure devices. He was a man of parts. In Zaragoza he worked as a gilder. In Fuendetodos —where his wife's relatives owned the house where his son was born—he worked the stony ground for what little there was to be got from it. José reminds one of the cheerful workers Goya painted later on, holding the leather wine bottle at arm's length so that the red stream of rioja accurately strikes the center of the mouth. There was a genial improvidence about him that is laconically expressed in the final record: *No testó porque no tenia de que:* He made no will because he had nothing to make a will about.

Gracia Lucientes had pretensions. And they were crested. She was an *hidalga*—a daughter of some one—descended from the nobility of Aragon. It was a claim appropriate to the country in that century. Every village in Spain had its Gracia Lucientes. The peninsula swarmed with thousands of authentic nobles and tens of thousands who dreamed of coats of arms on small walls. She was an excellent mother, and Goya showed a wandering son's deep affection for her.

In later times people who wanted to spade up for an illustrious painter the dubious traces of armorial quarterings could look to Gracia Lucientes. Those who would see his peasant wit and strength and shrewdness could look to José Goya.

They lived in no splendor. The house in Fuendetodos where Goya was born was on the Calle de la Alhondiga below the church that thumbs the sky at the top of the hill. It was made of stone set in rough, uneven lines and the walls were thick against the blazing heat of summer in Aragon and the long, stingingly cold winter.

When you stood in the street outside the house you could touch the walls on either side with outstretched hands. A step went down to the one large pole-beamed room on the first floor. There was an enormous fireplace, with two stone benches on either side, and a smaller room of stone—the kitchen—behind it. Upstairs, where Goya was born, there were two alcoves. The window had a heavy wooden shutter with a smaller shutter in that, and no glass at all. Behind that there was a storeroom, where sausages hung from the slanted roof and grain stood in yellow cones on the stone floor.

José Goya's family added half a dozen to a village population of less than a hundred and fifty people. Goya had two brothers, Tomás and Camillo, and a sister, Rita. Tomás followed the irregular occupations of his father. Rita married and went to live in Zaragoza. Camillo became a priest. He appeared in Madrid in the days of his brother's prosperity, and through him got a pleasant benefice at Chinchón, not far from Madrid, in country where Goya liked to go hunting.

Fuendetodos was a village without great variety, primitive and hard, an episode of the landscape of sweeping hills on whose summits forts from Roman and from Moorish days crumbled in the sunlight. Few stage-coaches rocked down the road from Zaragoza, in Goya's day, and the village has not yet entered the railroad era. There is no stream in Fuendetodos, and the land is rocky under the plow. In harvest time the village is colored yellow by threshed wheat. What wealth there was to be had from the village went to the landlord of those parts, the Conde de Fuentes, or to the coffers of piety.

Goya, playing in those steep streets as a child, survived a training that is rigorous because there is nothing but rigor as a weapon of survival in that country. What makes the Aragonese stubborn and proud is the country he lives in. New England's rock-strewn farms are tropical by comparison. The basis of picturesqueness in Aragon is scarcity—scarcity of water, of pasture, of trees, of everything but rocks. The people of Aragon learn early to take bread from stones.

2

MANY of the tales about Goya's youth are innocent enough. Perhaps the earliest is the story of how his drawing first attracted attention; it could not be more conservative. Indeed, it was being told about artists when Giotto was young.

One day the parish priest of Fuendetodos saw a boy drawing on a wall with a piece of burnt stick and the boy was Goya and the drawing was a pig. The priest was impressed.

"That is a very good drawing, my lad."

"Thank you, father."

"Who taught you to draw?"

"No one."

"You have no drawing teacher?"

"I have none, father."

This might go on for some time: at the expense of a certain lack of variety in the dialogue. But the tale—which we need not believe for a moment—tells that Goya was sent, at the priest's generous insistence, to a drawing school in Zaragoza.

It is an idle tale and venerable in the chronicle of art. What Goya first drew in Fuendetodos can scarcely have been memorable. There is more plausibility to the story that Goya's drawing attracted the attention of the Conde de Fuentes, and that he sent Goya to school in Zaragoza. But there is no certainty of that, either, and the obvious fact that Goya's father was a gilder, and therefore familiar with what opportunities there were for one who showed talent in art, must take precedence in importance when one looks for the early influences that shaped Goya's destiny.

Goya was high-spirited and unruly as a boy. When Zapater[1] went to Fuendetodos to gather his curious and exasperating and indispensable notes, the ancients told him that. They also remembered—with the pat appropriateness of all legends about celebrities—that young Goya used to sketch pictures around the village. And that he painted there.

Of Goya's earliest painting, only one trace remains, the curtains painted on either side of the chapel of relics in the parish church, and the picture of the Virgin of Pilar—the famous patron saint of the whole countryside—on the retablo.

[1] Francisco Zapater y Gómez: *Goya; Noticias biográficas.* Zaragoza: 1868.

Just before Franco's rebellion, I saw those paintings, and I should not have said they were by Goya if I saw them anywhere else on earth but in his native village. They are extraordinarily inert and uninspired. Goya himself took a skeptical view of the theory that he had painted them. When he went back to Fuendetodos in 1808, during the siege of Zaragoza, they were shown to him. He looked at the Virgin of Pilar and exclaimed: "You'd never say I painted that!"

The flagrant stories of young Goya's romantic escapades were overdrawn enough; Zapater set out to disprove them on grounds of piety. The same ancients—Cenon Grasa, 76 years old when Zapater talked to him in the eighteen sixties, Vicenta Grasa, 70, and Tomás Cortes, 73—had other tales to tell. Zapater says they knew Goya. But when did they know Goya? They must have been born in the seventeen nineties, when Goya was half a lifetime away from Fuendetodos. They must have been in their teens when Goya—by that time resoundingly celebrated—went back to Fuendetodos. Most of what they knew about his childhood was obviously hearsay romanticized by time. Cenon's grandfather was a friend of Goya. That is a link, but tenuous enough when one tries to compare it to what one knows about one's own grandfather's friends. Zapater speaks of a diary in which various members of the same Fuendetodos family had put down the memorable events of the neighborhood in the course of a century. That diary would be worth seeing. It might tell us something of the life of Fuendetodos during the dozen years Goya lived there. For when he was about thirteen the Goyas went to live in the famous provincial capital of Zaragoza.

3

THE brawls, the lovemaking and the swordplay of those years are all legendary, all shadows cast by the lengthening stature of his reputation. Street fights between the youths of rival parishes in Zaragoza were apt to be sanguinary. Knives were useful at night. Yriarte was one of the first to gather the tales of Goya as a young warrior in Zaragoza. Goya is supposed—and no bondsmen support that supposing—to have been the leader of a turbulent crowd that lived around Pilar Cathedral. They fought other gangs of roving youths around the town.

It is a plausible enough legend, appropriate to the country and the age and the character of Goya. But when it becomes circumstantial, it becomes vulnerable. When it is said that the death of three youths in a fight with the gang from the parish of San Luis caused Goya to flee to Madrid, then Zapater—who was interested anyway in giving Goya a more sedate reputation—can refute the legend by pointing out that the parish of San Luis was not yet in existence. Goya may have left Zaragoza because he had made himself unpopular with the Inquisitors. Or he may have left Zaragoza simply because he wanted to go to Madrid.

Zaragoza, John Langdon-Davies once remarked, is the ugliest town but one in Spain. "The Ebro has carved out a canyon in mud, and out of mud human beings have built a dust-coloured city." The rigor of that judgment was tempered for at least one other traveller there by the courtesy of the people who showed him all the surviving works and associations of Goya.

Zaragoza, on the Ebro, the Salduba of the Iberians, the Cæsaraugustea of the Romans, immemorially important as a trading center between France and Barcelona and Madrid, is the capital of Aragon not only in fact but also in spirit.

It is in Zaragoza that one sees concentrated the Aragonese character. There—in past years, at least—one found, as Havelock Ellis expressed it, a people who seemed "set apart from the rest of the world, of curiously firm and hard temper, tenacious of their own personal independence, and indifferent to the judgment of others. An Aragonese woman at prayer, with her dramatic and self-forgetful gestures, and an Aragonese couple dancing their national *jota*, with its ecstatic fury of concentrated muscular energy so utterly unlike any Andalusian dance, alike manifest a temperament of very special force and originality."[1]

It was out of this Aragonese temperament that Goya's character was formed. In all his work in Madrid he may seem to be a Madrileño, but first of all he is a man of Aragon. And being a painter from Aragon he was all the better equipped to see and understand and satirize the airs of the court at Madrid.

Zapater suggests that Goya lived in Zaragoza from the time he was thirteen to the time he was twenty. But Sanchez Cantón has shown that he was in Madrid from time to time in the course of those years. The long journey through Aragon and across Castile along heroically bad eighteenth-century roads by carriage or on muleback was not one to be undertaken casually; he must have lived in Madrid for months on end before returning to Zaragoza.

[1]*The Soul of Spain.* By Havelock Ellis. Boston: Houghton Mifflin Company. 1915.

4

WHEN he looked back to Zaragoza long afterwards, it was with a mixture of rancor and affection. The rancor was caused by the battles over the decorations for Pilar. The affection was for the friends and pleasures of his youth.

His best friend, Martin Zapater y Clavería, was a school-mate of the Zaragoza days. It was to Zapater that Goya wrote the series of letters that are the most important personal running commentary of his life. Goya and Zapater went to a school run in Zaragoza by Father Joaquin. His letters show what we might have suspected, that he was not a singularly devout scholar. His spelling alone is enough to bring on a Castilian grammarian's funeral. Yet in a time when literacy itself was uncommon, Goya's ability to read and write was distinguished, comparatively speaking. And from his records of financial accounts it is fair to say he was well above the average for his time in mathematics.

The money José Goya made as a gilder supported the family. And although one would be glad to find evidence that José had wealth enough to have sold two houses to raise funds for Goya's journey to Rome, as one eminent writer believes, one is unable to discover it. There was enough money to send Goya to Luzan's art classes. But the evidence available indicates that his studies there were paid for by friends of the family, who saw that Goya had the makings of an artist in him.

Casanova, who went to Zaragoza a few years later, speaks of it as the sort of town an artist would enjoy. His descriptions sound mildly like a Venetian's dream of Spain. "Long cloaks and low hats were to be seen at every corner. They looked like dark phantoms more than men, for the cloak covered up at least half the face. Underneath the cloak was carried *el espadin*, a sword of enormous length. Persons who wore this costume were treated with enormous respect, though they were arrant rogues mostly; still they might be powerful noblemen in disguise."[1] Since he had recently had some trouble with the Inquisition himself, he was pleased with the tales he heard in Zaragoza about Pignatelli, president of the Zaragoza Inquisition, a man, Casanova said solemnly, who always had the girl he had slept with thrown out in the morning, and the procuress who had obtained her imprisoned.

The bullfights, Casanova thought, were much better in Zaragoza than in Madrid. He was scarcely an authority. But it is an interesting observation in the light of Goya's lifelong interest in bullfighting. Young Spaniards learned about bullfighting very early. Goya painted them at their game, in one of the tapestry cartoons: one child holding a wicker effigy of a bull over his head while the others take turns with the wooden sword and the ragged muleta. They do not stop with that safe and sane version, even in childhood. They practice on any horned cattle they can find, showing an expertness and an indifference to danger that is impressive. The ablest and the bravest take part in novilladas wherever they can find them. And in the main bullrings they risk imprisonment by jumping into the ring when the guards are not looking before risking the more welcome perils of the fight itself. At Malaga three or four years ago a boy of twelve

[1]*The Memoirs of Jacques Casanova.* Translated by Arthur Machen. A. & C. Boni.

jumped into the ring with a stick and a ragged muleta when
Belmonte, Lalanda and Barrera were fighting before the
Caliph of Spanish Morocco, who was being honored by the
Spanish government of that year for reasons best known to
history. The boy did several passes before the bull beauti-
fully while the crowd roared and the Guardias Civiles (holding their jangling swords with that pain-in-the-groin gesture
as they ran) sprinted after him, once the men of the cuadrillas had got the bull away. Belmonte went over and put his
arm over the boy's shoulder, which was probably accolade
enough for him. Then they led him out, and every one set-
tled back to see less exciting torearing. The Spanish crowds
used to call those boys *millionarios*.

José's profession would carry him to the studios of the
Zaragozan painters, to the churches and the palaces and the
convents and the great secular and ecclesiastical offices where
there were paintings to be framed, frames to be gilded. His
work was with the work of artists. He would think of his son,
who had shown a talent for drawing. He would speak of it;
he would look for ways to encourage his son. Goya very likely
went with his father. Viñaza has suggested that José's occupation led him to place his son in the studio of some
good artist. At any rate, to place him in the studio of some
painter.

For it is obvious that José's occupation had a part in shap-
ing Goya's career. As Sanchez Cantón has said: "Mais ni la
révélation du prêtre, ni la perspicacité du Comte de Fuentes,
seigneur de Fuendetodos et amateur d'art, ne réussissent a
expliquer la vocation artistique de l'enfant aussi bien que le
fait d'être né au foyer d'un homme qui n'était pas étranger au

dessin et a ses finesses."[1] That, it seems to me, is the core of the matter, all contrary opinions notwithstanding.

It is possible—and, on the whole, desirable—to dismiss Luzan as an artist; it would be injudicious to ignore his influence on Goya. For one of the astonishing things about Goya is that he came out of one of the dullest, most lamentable periods of Spain's art. Luzan, who was Goya's first teacher, had his share in making the period mediocre. He was one of the influences Goya spent some time outgrowing. It is clear from the perspective of the present day. In fact, it seems astonishing that Goya ever outgrew the successive blights of Luzan and the ineffable Mengs at all. There was plenty of work for artists to do. But Spanish artists were not held in high esteem. The Bourbons had imported foreign painters to decorate their palaces. Carpetbaggers of Europe's thrones, they came from other countries and brought painters from abroad. Spaniards who painted were expected to paint as they did. The greatness of Goya is that he finally broke through those restraints. But that did not happen for a long time.

José Luzan was a fairly important figure in Spain's art at the time. Beruete, who dismisses him as "a master of some standing who had formed himself in Italy in that period of facile mannerism," believes it is safe to say that he made no impression on Goya's art. On the contrary, it seems to me, he made a good deal of impression on Goya's art. Until he was forty he painted pretty much in a style that the Luzans of the day made possible. Indeed, Beruete himself says that in 1783, when Goya was nearly thirty-seven, "this man, who

[1] F. J. Sanchez Cantón: *Goya*. G. Cres et Cie. Paris.

was to become one of the greatest portraitists of the world, had not, up to that date, made a single striking portrait, nor one in which appeared those individual qualities which he was to show later." Luzan had not only been a court painter in Madrid under Philip V but artistic censor to the Inquisition. There is something to be said for Stokes's praise of Luzan's thoroughness. He made his pupils copy engravings for a long time before he would let them draw from plaster casts, and there they were kept an even longer period before they were allowed to draw from live models. Certainly the years spent in Luzan's academy affected Goya.

5

IT IS a part of the undying legend of Goya that he fled Zaragoza and went down to Madrid as the upshot of a brawl, with the alguacils and the Inquisition hot after him, bent on throwing him into a dungeon. The tale is one of a magnificent chain. It is the recurring motivation forever used to move Goya from one place to another.

He is not allowed to travel until he has fought. When he leaves Fuendetodos and goes to Zaragoza it is said to be the result of a brawl. When he leaves Zaragoza and goes to Madrid—less than two hundred miles away, yet far removed in time and mountain travel—it is said to be the result of more desperate adventure in the dark. When he leaves Madrid and goes to Rome it is written that he went because one morning he was found in a narrow street with a dagger in his back, and the Inquisitors were after him. Surely an odd incentive to study art around the Vatican. And the superbly told affair of the lovely nun brings him back from Rome.

Now it is idle, not to say priggish, to disbelieve stories about Goya simply because they are romantic. The one reason, the one sound reason, for not believing these tales is that there is nothing to prove them true. Goya, having got so far in his work at Zaragoza, would naturally want to go on to Madrid, to look for the fair rewards and to see the world. The principal commissions in painting came from the Church and the Court in Madrid. And the most influential body in Spain's art, the Academy of San Fernando, was in Madrid.

All painters in Spain wanted to go there. Other painters from Zaragoza had gone to Madrid from Luzan's school. Francisco Bayeu, Goya's future brother-in-law and his lifelong antagonist in matters of art, had a studio in Madrid, where Goya worked from time to time. When Goya entered the competition at Parma he said, for want of any one better to mention, that he was a pupil of Vayeu—that was the way he spelled it—and the only time he could have studied under Bayeu was in these years.

Toward the end of 1763, when he was seventeen, Goya took part in a competition at the Academy of San Fernando. Sanchez Cantón found that in the Academy's records, which show that Goya's training under Luzan was not remarkably successful. He got no prize. Nor did he shine in another competition in the following year. That time, Bayeu's younger brother Ramón, who was Goya's age, was the winner. And two years later Goya was no better in the eyes of the academicians.

His talent in that time may have been devoted to the pleasures of Madrid. In the capital he was not isolated. There was a strong Aragonese party at court, headed by the Count of

Aranda, and Goya found friends among them. They were useful at first. But in Madrid he was at home from the beginning, and he soon found friends of his own.

In the most urbane of all sketches of Goya, Sir William Rothenstein said: "That indifference to injustice, which allows young painters to lead such calm and dignified lives in England, was absent from Goya's anarchical nature. His desire for freedom of thought and action soon earned him a dangerous reputation; and his father, afraid lest his son might fall into the clutches of the Inquisition, then still in the full force of its existence, managed to send him to Madrid. The jealous mistrust which exceptional intelligence seems not uncommonly to sow in the minds of foolish people soon made Madrid equally dangerous for Goya; the many escapades of which he was accused were as likely as not the subject of considerable exaggeration." They were indeed. And they have no more substance now than the legend that Goya went on his way to study art in Rome as a member of a wandering bullfighter's *cuadrilla.*

6

Goya's reticence about his Roman days has been a source of despondency to scholars and a happy challenge to the inventiveness of fabulists.

Late eighteenth-century Rome was powerful in art, picturesque in life, turbulent, decadent and lawless. To place Goya in relation to the roaring life of the time is as simple as it would be to place some young painter of our day in relation to the most spectacular events in Manhattan during these strange years of grace. Even the usually tranquil Stokes[1] has Goya fighting his way through the crowds around the Forum on the day in 1769 when the monk Ganganelli, newly chosen Pope Clement XIV, rode his white palfrey through the streets attended by Swiss Guards in yellow and black.

Of course Goya may not have seen the show. But on his behalf it is easy to see through Silvagni's eyes "the balconies filled with ladies whose beauty was thought to be enhanced by powder and patches; the façades of every palace on the route covered with priceless tapestries and carpets of the most exquisite textures; the Palazzo Colonna decorated with trophies of arms captured in past days from the Turks; the banner of the northern republic flying above the Palazzo Venezia; the houses of the Doria, the Asti, the Cenci, the Malatesta, and a score of like noble names, enriched with hangings of red damask and gold lace." And so on. That is all appropriate to Goya. So is the more doubtful remark that "Rome was the first city in the world, and its citizens were proudly conscious of the advantages they had to offer. Society was brilliantly cosmopolitan, and the peculiar conditions of the Papal States intensified an atmosphere of culture and luxury to which Europe could show no equal." Gibbon, who had been in Rome three or four years earlier, took a less impressionable view of Rome's contemporary glories; in his eyes the decline and fall were notably evident.

As Mr. Low, his most recent biographer, remarks, Gibbon surveyed the scene with a practical eye,[2] and though "his

[1]*Francisco Goya.* By Hugh Stokes. G. P. Putnam's Sons. 1914.
[2]*Edward Gibbon: 1737–1794.* By D. M. Low. Random House.

canvas is both mellow and trenchant," he found that "In Rome the voice of freedom and discord is no longer heard; and instead of the foaming torrent, a smooth and stagnant lake reflects the image of idleness and servitude." Gibbon said—in a passage that Mr. Low has admirably shortened and that I shall shorten further: "The first and most natural root of a great city is the labour and populousness of the adjacent country. But the greater part of the Campagna of Rome is reduced to a dreary and desolate wilderness: the overgrown estates of the princes and the clergy are cultivated by the lazy hands of indigent and hopeless vassals; and the scanty harvests are confined or exported for the benefit of a monopoly. A second and more artificial cause of the growth of a metropolis is the residence of a monarch, the expense of a luxurious court, and the tribute of dependent provinces. Those provinces and tributes had been lost in the fall of the empire; and if some streams of the silver of Peru and the gold of Brazil have been attracted by the Vatican, the revenues of the cardinals, the fees of office, the oblations of pilgrims and clients, and the remnant of ecclesiastical taxes, afford a poor and precarious supply, which maintains, however, the idleness of the court and city. The population of Rome, far below the measure of the great capitals of Europe, does not exceed one hundred and seventy thousand inhabitants; and within the spacious enclosure of the walls, the largest portion of the seven hills is overspread with vineyards and ruins. The beauty and splendour of the modern city may be ascribed to the abuses of the government, to the influence of superstition. Each reign (the exceptions are rare) has been marked by the rapid elevation of a new family, enriched by the childless pontiff at the expense of the church and country. The palaces of these fortunate nephews are the most costly monuments of elegance and servitude: the perfect arts of architecture, painting and sculpture, have been prostituted in their service; and the galleries and gardens are decorated with the most precious works of antiquity." Gibbon, whose "conversation was with the dead rather than the living," was not apt to overpraise the Rome that may have been only a shadow of its former greatness to him, but to Goya it may have been a place of considerable wonder and pleasure.

Goya's stay in Rome was not very long, and his serious study was not very arduous. Of all the adventures there no sound record survives and for all the painting he is supposed to have done—the oddest that has been ascribed to him is scenes of Spanish life to sell to homesick Spaniards—not one remains.

In after years he said only that he had studied in Rome: and—what was more—that he had paid his own way. This distinguished him from other painters who went to Rome under the patronage of the nobility or the paternalism of the academies. Goya may have had some one particularly in mind when he spoke of paying his own way. Some one he did not like very much. Bayeu had studied in Luzan's classes in Zaragoza, he studied in Rome before establishing himself in Madrid.

And the one contemporary record of Goya's Italian journey—the *Mercure de France's* notation that he had got second prize in a competition of the Academy of Parma—says that Goya was a pupil of Bayeu "painter to the King of Spain." Goya himself never, so far as one can find, mentioned that episode in Parma. Did he go to Parma for the award? And where is the painting he did, a scene of Hannibal, victorious, looking at Italy from the Alps?

Goya might have won the first prize, the committee remarked, if he had just paid a little more serious attention to composition and made his colors more natural. Whatever natural means. The sermonette on composition is certainly familiar. It may even have reminded Goya of the long mornings in Luzan's Zaragozan classes.

If we recall that in those years there were fairly close relations between the court of Spain and the court of Parma, through members of the royal families who went back and forth like company representatives, the idea suggests itself that Goya may have gone to Parma through their influence. And Goya's explicit statement that he paid his own way to Italy certainly points to the contrary. It must be emphasized that we do not know the date he went to Italy. Knowing that he was back in Zaragoza at the end of 1771, Beruete's affirmation that it was in 1770 is the soundest. He then returned to Spain in the following year.

7

How did Goya travel from Madrid to Rome? The legend is that he joined a wandering bullfighter's cuadrilla and with the matadores, the picadores and all the rag-tag-and-bobtail of a vagabond troupe went from town to town across the bleak high plain of Castile, stopping to give bullfights in village bullrings or barricaded plazas, sometimes winning the approval of the crowd and gathering in enough money to give every one all the wine and wenching he wanted, sometimes

being booed out when the bulls were bad and the luck was out, and so over the mountains and down the richer plain to the Mediterranean coast. There, with what pesetas he had managed to save, he found passage on some sea-galled sloop bound for Italy.

It is a generous tribute to the character of Goya that so many romantic gestures are ascribed to him. He might have gone to Italy by slow and for the times comparatively peaceful land travel across the Pyrenees and France. Though that itself would probably become an odyssey of dark encounters, episodes in mountain inns, battles with brigands and so on, before the tale was over.

Time and many commentaries have crowded the calendar of Goya's Roman journey. He would obviously have had little time to paint if he were to do all the things, carry out all the exploits that are gathered in the leyenda Goyesca.

Whether he found boon companions among the French students of art at the Villa Medici or the supposedly staider young Englishmen, it is easier to fit Goya's temperament to the scene than to find proof of the escapades. One may enjoy the story that Goya, "proud, vainglorious and foolhardy," climbed perilously around the shaky cornice of the tomb of Cecilia Metella, without going so far along the Iriarte-Matheron road as Stokes is willing to go when he suggests that "perhaps it was this same monument he clambered up to cut his name above that of Vanloo. 'What a Frenchman can do, a Spaniard ought also to do,' was his boast. Vanloo as Court painter to Philip V could have been but a name to him, but the ill-feeling of this foreign appointment still rankled among Spanish artists. Upon a third occasion he climbed up to the lantern of the dome of St. Peter's to cut his name upon a stone no man had reached since the builders had struck their scaffolding. There was a story that Poussin had tried to perform the same deed, and Goya, full of patriotism, wished to surpass him. The feat was perhaps rendered less perilous by the little iron foot supports for the use of the workmen who decorated the dome at Easter, but their task was always recognized as one of extreme danger. There was an emulous spirit abroad at this period, when every young soul aspired to the skies. Von Loga draws a parallel between Goya at Rome and Goethe scaling the steeple at Strasbourg, almost in the same year."[1]

Goya is supposed to have painted a portrait of the Pope in Rome. But since no trace of the painting itself can be found, and since there is a good deal of discrepancy over just which Pope he painted, one is reluctant to believe that story.

And one is even more reluctant to disbelieve, on the other hand, the story that Goya knew the painter David in Rome. Not only because they should have known each other, but because in some of Goya's early pictures there were traces of David's influence in the precise, sharp painting. Even Rothenstein believed that in Rome Goya "saw much of David, with whom he corresponded later in life, and whose revolutionary ideas strengthened his own convictions." But so far as one has been able to discover, Goya not only did not see David in Rome but he could not have seen him. David was not there at the time.

One of the most interesting tales about Goya's stay in Rome is the story that Catherine the Great's ambassador tried to

[1]Stokes. *Op. cit.*

get him to go to St. Petersburg. That would certainly have led to confrontations worth hearing about. Consider Goya's reputation. And consider Great Catherine's. And think of them together.

The final escapade in Rome ascribed to Goya finds him caught *in flagrante*, climbing the wall of a convent on his way to see a beautiful nun. Iriarte would have us believe he was thrown into a dungeon. His situation was desperate. He was in a fair way to be executed. Fortunately, so the tale tells, the Spanish ambassador successfully intervened. Goya was released, on condition that he should leave Rome forever. He did leave Rome, soon enough. And, as it turned out, it was forever.

III

A Painter from Aragon

[1772–1789]

III

A Painter from Aragon
[1772–1789]

I

ONCE back in Spain from that Roman holiday the next
thing to do was to establish himself as a painter. His efforts
so far had not been conspicuously successful. He had no
precocity. In fact it is interesting to notice that the tales of
Goya's precocity are told about his childhood—the period we
know least.

It wasn't that he was ahead of his time, by any means. He
was, if anything, behind it. His brushwork was competent,
his design was rudimentary and wooden, his color was lusterless. That's the brutal truth. You may look at some of his early
work and see traces in it of genius to come. But you would not
find it—or look for it—if he had died with nothing else to show.

Goya's early struggles were with himself, not with outer
adversity; if he got no early recognition it was—even in a
spectacularly mediocre period of art for great Spain—because
there was nothing in particular to recognize. He had to
develop a style before it could be recognized. And once he had
developed it far enough to stand out it was recognized and
the fair rewards followed.

He never stopped developing. He became one of the two
or three greatest painters Spain ever had, a master by the stand-

ards of the world. To the end of his days he was still learning, still going forward.

The economic struggle was pressing, but not desperate. A man born in an Aragonese village and bred in that stiff tradition can live a long time with some bread and some meat and a *bota* full of wine.

To go on as a painter he had to have commissions. He had to look to the two sources: the Church and the Court. It took some time to get any attention from a court ruled by Charles III, who imported his painters from other countries. And though life in Madrid was far more appealing, what commissions Goya got at first from the Church were more easily to be had in Zaragoza, where the competition was not so keen, and where Goya was known. So for the first few years after his return from Rome he worked frequently in Zaragoza.

Mayer believes he was in Zaragoza again by the time he was twenty-six. "In October 1771 he was back again in Zaragoza. He was commissioned to paint the small choir of the chapel of the Virgen del Pilar in the Pilar Cathedral and on October 21, 1771, he laid his designs before the Board of Works. During the next few years we find the artist employed as a fresco painter at and near Zaragoza; but after a while he got tired of his Aragonese home and went back to Madrid. This move seems to have been made at the beginning of the year 1775. As in it Francisco Bayeu is mentioned as his brother-in-law he must have been married at this time. He lived at no. 66 Carrera de S. Jeronimo, in the house of the Marquesa de Campollano, with his young wife."[1]

[1]*Francisco de Goya.* By August L. Mayer. Translated by Robert West. London: J. M. Dent.

Sanchez Cantón points out that Mayer cited the *Moniteur* for 1771 for the Parma award. Others say the *Mercure* for 1772. Which is not merely confusing. It doesn't make sense. But he agrees on the date of the Pilar commission. He believes the Aula Dei frescoes were done in 1771 and 1772, which, it seems, is placing the dates a year or two early if Goya waited, as it is reasonable to suppose, until after the Pilar work was over before going out to Aula Dei to begin the rather extensive work there. It was, at any rate, a fairly busy time for Goya. He had other walls to fill with images as religious as his somewhat impious hands could make them at the Sobradiel palace in Zaragoza and at the church of Remolinos. Between that time and the beginning of his work on the tapestry cartoons in Madrid Goya may have gone back to the capital several times. And at one point, certainly, he married the tranquil Josefa. Yet, characteristically, there is no record of the date of Goya's marriage. He presents the biographer a fait accompli in mentioning his first son.

At the beginning of September, 1775, when he was not yet thirty, Goya wrote a letter. What he said in it was not so important as that it was from Madrid, where he was at last established, and that it was to his old friend of the early Zaragoza days, the genial and astute Martin Zapater y Claverias.

It is the earliest letter that we know of in a correspondence that was to last for the rest of the eighteenth century. These letters[1] are an enormously illuminating record of what Goya thought and what Goya did in those turbulent years. He wrote Zapater with the candor a man feels toward a friend

[1]*Goya, Noticias Biográficas.*

in the town he came from, a man he'd known in school, a man who was his liaison between Madrid and old companions and various relatives in Zaragoza.

"I'm glad to hear you're enjoying yourself and that you've seen Francisco," Goya said. Francisco was Bayeu. "I've noted all you said about the work, and it will be best if you don't think any more about it. I'm grateful to you and I haven't time to tell you more now, except that I have the St. Christopher and on the reverse I'll do the Dolores and send it to you."

2

For a thousand people who have heard about Goya and the lovely Duchess of Alba there may be one who knows about his wife. To say that there is not much to know is only to make a biographical detail of necessity. Zapater does not mention her until 1777, when Goya was "already married and the father of a fine boy."

Her name was Josefa. Goya called her La Pepa, when he spoke of one of her punctual childbearings. She had a bad time with them—of their twenty children only one survived Goya. She was a sister of the Bayeus. In the natural course of events he would meet her at their house in Zaragoza. He married her after he got back from Rome. There is no more reason to suppose that simple propinquity made a husband out of Goya than there is to suppose that because of the objections of her brother Francisco—who always looked at Goya with a somewhat beady eye—they romantically eloped.

Indeed, if we were to devote ourselves to supposition, there are more interesting fields. What did La Pepa think of Goya's

he Collection of Jules S. Bache   DON MANUEL OSORIO

JOSEFA BAYEU, WIFE OF GO

art? Did she say anything when she saw the savage jokes he made about marriage in the *Caprichos?* Was she there when he decided that a painting of Jupiter devouring his children with the air of a god picking a drumstick would make a good decoration for the dining room of his house on the other side of the Manzanares?

He speaks of her in his letters to Zapater from time to time. It is not always about La Pepa's tragically futile fruitfulness. He worries about her health, sends her regards back to the old friends in Zaragoza, quotes her remarks.

When Goya goes to Arenas to stay with the Infante Don Luis, La Pepa does not go along. The Infante, however, remembers her. "A dress for my wife all made of gold and silver and worth thirty thousand reales," he writes Zapater, is one of the presents given to Goya.

It was not usual in the eighteenth century for Spanish wives to accompany their husbands when their husbands went out. Indeed, it was not usual in the century that followed, or in the first part of the century after that.

The Duchess of Alba, who entertained Goya rather more often than she entertained Goya's wife, sent presents to La Pepa. It is a part of the legend that she sent her the sort of things to eat that are always referred to as delicacies from her table, and that the footmen were told, according to custom, to leave the gold dishes as presents.

Goya's portrait of La Pepa shows a woman who looks rather retiring, who has a tranquil dignity, and who is about as far as possible from the popular idea of the dark, opulent Spanish type. Her hair is reddish gold piled high and ringed with a braid, her figure thin, her eyes wide apart and intelligent and thoughtful. She is dressed for the occasion; one feels that the occasion is a rare one.

It is as though she had a Zaragozan reticence in the worldly atmosphere of Charles IV and Maria Luisa's Madrid. For in Zaragoza she was among her own people, a sister of the Bayeus, and completely at ease. In Madrid she was the wife of Goya. And that was a somewhat demanding part to play.

3

MENGS was the chilling autocrat of painting in Madrid. He was extremely influential, and his influence was extraordinarily bad. He approved Goya's painting cartoons for the palace tapestries, but he did not approve of Goya. What he did for Goya's advancement was little, what he did to hold Goya back in the growth of his natural, forceful style did him no good, though it was not a permanent harm. Mengs had perfected a facile sterility, Goya was still developing a profound vitality, when Mengs passed from Spain. Fortunately, none of the seven Mengs children Charlès III pensioned took their father's gloomy place.

When Charles III called Mengs to Madrid in 1762 to decorate the enormous new palace and generally take charge of art for the next fourteen years, he already had a considerable reputation in Europe. His full name was Antony Raphael Mengs, but he insisted on being called Raphael Mengs because he found the allusion reassuring. He was born in Bohemia, and his nationality was as eclectic as his art. His father, Ismael, was a Danish painter who had been an artist for the elector of Saxony. Ismael took Antony Raphael to

Rome, where he proceeded to become a Catholic, and, by the time he was twenty-seven, director of the Vatican's painting school.

Mengs developed meticulously scholastic theories of art. It is fair to say they are the sort of antiquity-haunted principles art employs when, suffering from plastic anemia, it has least vitality and invention of its own. Winckelmann, the famous eighteenth-century pundit of classicism, was the friend of Mengs. They studied Greek and Roman art together. They told living artists sadly that they could never surpass the artists long under the headstones, all they could do was to imitate them.

That was the doctrine Mengs brought to Spain. He said painting should be inspired by the venerable classic artists, with a strong tincture of Titian and Raphael. Naturally, we all learn from the past; but Mengs wanted to move into it. He believed in such lifeless decorousness that he developed a desperately stylized mannerism. He was against using bright colors. What talent he had—and Mengs had talent, unquestionably—was frozen. As Reinach said, "He was led astray by the fatal seductions of eclecticism, which knows beauty only at second hand." It is one of Reinach's most felicitous epitaphs in that incomparable book full of lively obituaries for art's illustrious dead.

Nothing could be more alien to the vigorous genius of Goya. Yet these were the rules he had to hurdle to paint in Madrid. He got over them—but it was a waste of time and spirit. Goya wanted to paint what he saw as he alone saw it, not as a man from Aragon might think a committee composed of some Greeks, some Romans, and the ghosts of Raphael and

Titian might see a pretty *maja* on the Prado or Pepe-Hillo killing his second bull in the Easter corrida in Madrid.

Inviting Mengs to take charge of art in Spain was welcoming a blight. There are touches of the blight in some of the portraits of Charles III and others Goya painted in the time of Mengs. Goya, fortunately, went on to paint so many more portraits that he could afford to take the Mengs hurdle on the way. But it is preposterous to say that it was good for Goya.

Casanova's malicious recollections of Mengs in Madrid show what a fatuous sort of pedant Goya had to face. The Venetian knew Mengs in Rome as well as in Spain. He found him pretentious, didactic, rather pompous and inclined to hate all other living painters. "He was an ignorant man and liked to pass for a scholar; he sacrificed to Bacchus and Comus and would fain be thought sober; he was lustful, bad-tempered, envious and miserly, but yet would be considered a virtuous man."[1]

The escapades of Casanova in Madrid put Mengs in mortal fear for his own reputation. And it is apparent that the chevalier took an unholy pleasure in baiting him. Casanova made fun of him for thinking that the remains of the Tower of Babel still existed, for knowing four languages and speaking them all badly, and for saying he wished he were Raphael. When Mengs beat his children with a stick, saying that was the way his father had made a great painter of him, Casanova would have none of that pedagogy. "He died at the age of fifty," Casanova remarks, "and is regarded by posterity as a stoic philosopher, a scholar and a compendium of all the

[1]*The Memoirs of Jacques Casanova.* Translated by Arthur Machen.

virtues and this opinion must be ascribed to a fine biography of him in royal quarto, choicely printed and dedicated to the King of Spain." Certainly it cannot be ascribed to Jacques Casanova.

4

GOYA's popular success was assured when he began to paint the tapestry cartoons. They were admired in his time, and they have been admired ever since for their glowing color and gayety. They have the beautiful quality of being every one's idea of what Spanish life should be like in the best of all possible Spanish worlds. The peasant has never been able to afford quite such bright silks and satins, the grapes have never been so sweet, the wenches so fair.

It was in 1776 that Goya got the first commission. The royal tapestry looms at Santa Barbara were being given a new lease on life. The plan was to have typical Spanish scenes painted by the leading artists of the time, so that the weavers could copy them in tapestries for the royal palaces. Cruzada Villaamil has traced the story of the cartoons more thoroughly than any other man, from the time they were painted, through the years they lay in damp rolls rotting and forgotten, to their triumphal resurrection.

Goya painted tapestry cartoons from 1776 to 1791. With intervals. Sometimes the intervals were between orders. Other intervals were caused by Goya's laziness, or by his preoccupation with other amusements, other commissions for paintings.

You would not know the Goya of the stinging *Caprichos* and the furious *Desastres* from the bright scenes he painted for the tapestry weavers. They are painted with a Venetian gayety; the satire is gentle and the love of national scenes and customs is disarming. Some of them are anecdotes; for example, the painting of the card game under the trees, in which the winner's hatful of money is completely explained to every one except his opponent, who is unaware that the victor has an accomplice giving signals over his shoulder.

Life in them is largely a song. Girls dance around with men playing blind man's buff—a game that was at the moment extraordinarily fashionable: it is illuminating to know that Gibbon was playing it about the same time in Lausanne— children climb apple trees as nicely pruned as though they had been grown for the playground, and young blades follow young wenches down leafy paths with the most irresponsibly dishonorable intentions obvious in their attitudes.

Attitudes of Versailles are struck against the background of Castile. Peasants wear Petit Trianon costumes about their work, and the work seems to be carried out to the music of Haydn. A good deal of earnest debate has gone on as to whether Goya was the first to introduce the lives of the people into Spanish art with these cartoons. The question is preposterous. In the first place, Bayeu had already been doing the same sort of thing for some time before Goya started. And in the second place—which is more important—these pleasant paintings are no more true to the actual lives of the people of Spain in Goya's time than Watteau's *fêtes galantes* are true to the realities of eighteenth-century France.

Goya was pleased with the commission, however much he might grumble about the rate of payment, however much he might put off till well beyond the last minute the necessity for turning in his paintings. The tapestry weavers complained

THE STILT WALKERS — CARTOON FOR A TAPESTRY

LA VENDIMIA — CARTOON FOR A TAPEST

at times that he was making the pattern too intricate. At other times they went ahead on their own notion and left out subtleties Goya had painted in. Some of the tapestries woven from Goya's paintings were pale and laundered versions of his cartoons. But they carry a good deal of the original vitality. The royal rooms that held them were certainly made gayer for having Goya's pictures there.

They are, without question, glorifications of Spanish life. To say that in them country maidens are obviously duchesses dressed for the part is to miss the point somewhat: a few may be country maidens as Goya knew them—but they are dressed as duchesses, in Goya's time, seldom had the taste or the imagination, with one exception, to dress. That is why one may feel lenient to the theory that the Duchess of Alba appears in the *Maja con Los Embozados*. For though it is true that she was too young to have been there with those ruffians at all, she is too pretty not to have been the heroine of the adventure.

5

GOYA was ill in 1777. He had a tormenting attack of the curiously mysterious malady that has led art critics to write like physicians and physicians to write like art critics in their efforts to decide what illness Goya had.

It was in April, 1777, that he wrote Zapater thanking him for his good wishes for his health and assuring him that he need not doubt but that if he were to bore any one with the tale of his ailments he would choose Zapater. But thank God, he said, he was better, and he hoped that he had escaped for good. Though, as it turned out, he hadn't.

The etchings after Velasquez were made in 1778. They are among his earliest etchings, certainly, and decidedly they are not among his best. It is not for their qualities in art that they are significant. Neither Goya nor any one else would ever have made a reputation as an etcher for the series after Velasquez. They are, however, significant because Goya chose to make a series of etchings after the work of that particular artist. And the fact that he made them in the year of an illness sets another pattern. For it was always to be so. Full-blooded, restless, exasperated by anything that constrained his free movements or in any way held him down, Goya spent the times when he could not go out of his house for any length of time in furious work on the plates that were to become a great part of his celebrity in his time and his immortality later on.

He wrote Zapater in December, 1778, saying that he was sending him, by one Antonio Ibañez, a set of the works of Belazquez—so Goya spelled it, taking a usual Spanish freedom with the b and the v; and less unorthodox than many of his ways of spelling—"which I have engraved and which as you know are in the King's possession." He told Zapater he had had a good deal of trouble in getting them out, which certainly is easy to believe.

Yet they were not, really, worth it. Goya's etchings after Velasquez are sound, thorough, and pretty dull work. They are not very free impressions—though free in details—of paintings that are now known the world over. The marble-eyed young Prince Balthazar Carlos is the most famous of the sixteen. But they do not rise much above the level of copies made for souvenirs or for some other widespread distribution in the days before cameras. Mayer remarks rather aptly that "It is natural that an artist of his temperament could not and would not be an unselfish copyist, but Goya did not here take the decisive step of making his own style the thing of paramount importance." It would certainly be better if he had. As an unwitting judgment of their worth I remember once buying a single print of one of the *Caprichos* at the Calcografía Nacional in Madrid. It was still wet from the printing I had watched. And to guard it the courteous director wrapped it in an imperfect print of the Balthazar Carlos.

More significant than the value of Goya's etchings after Velasquez is the fact that he made them at all. In the first place, because it brought him to the careful study of his most famous predecessor. At the time the influence of Tiepolo and the dominance of Mengs—imported foreigners who made native Spaniards feel alien in the art of their own country— was strong at the court of Charles III. Mengs spoke well of Velasquez. But his praise had a flavor of patronage, for all his heroes were dead classics. Goya's discovery of Velasquez, as Sanchez Cantón calls it, at a time when that Spaniard's paintings by no means held first place among the paintings in the royal collections, certainly influenced his own work. The careful examination the making of the etchings required was a part of Goya's education in art.

Goya admired Velasquez. But it is a question whether he was attracted to him of his own volition or whether the making of the etchings was simply a commission. As he told Zapater, the set was in the King's possession. Even Mayer's resolution is indecisive. He makes some pother over deciding whether Godoy could have ordered them, "as Yriarte thinks and as Beruete does not quite deny" on the grounds that

Godoy was unimportant at court. This seems to draw an unnecessary distinction. In the first place, Godoy was playing his own game around the court some time before he burst into full arrogant power after Charles III's watchful eye over Maria Luisa, his amorous daughter-in-law, was gone. And in the second place, since Goya definitely told Zapater that King Charles III already had the set in 1778, Mayer's suggestion that Godoy could not have acquired the prints before 1793 is irrelevant. What is the use of saying that something we know had happened in 1778 could not have happened before 1793?

The principal reason for discussing the question is to trace Goya's slow progress toward the powerful job of court painter. It is apparent that the etchings helped. But neither the etchings nor the tapestry cartoons nor any other work that brought him before Charles III's eye was enough. He never made Goya court painter.

Goya's baptism in the cool stream of Velasquez had other results. Beruete, who as a partisan of Velasquez seems inclined to attach more importance to it than any one else, points out triumphantly that Goya was "employed to go through the royal collections of paintings, which until lately had been scattered in the Buen Retiro, San Lorenzo del Escorial, San Ildefonso, Aranjuez, the Casa de Campo, the Quinta del Duque del Arco, the Torre de la Parada, the Casa Palacio de las Batuecas, the Castillo de Viñuelas, and the Zarzuela." It was Charles III's idea to gather all the best paintings and bring them to the enormous new royal palace in Madrid.

That palace is one of the commanding royal residences of Europe. It is colossal even on that scale, a postmaster general's

dream of a building, enormous on the banks of the abashed
and inadequate Manzanares River. And the loot of art Goya
saw was the best of the grand manner. "There were to ·be
found," as Beruete says, "those portraits and subject paintings
of Titian which form the splendid and unique collection of
this master which we now possess, accompanied by other
Italian creations of the best period; there were the primitive
painters, generally belonging to the Flemish School, and those
of Rubens, Van Dyck, of Dürer, of Holbein and of Murillo,"
the Murillo Charles III's mother, Isabel Farnese, had vastly
admired when she went to Seville. Not to mention the
Frenchmen the Bourbons, Philip V and Ferdinand VI,
bought in expensive quantities.

And of them all, Beruete exultantly remarks, Goya chose
the works of Velasquez to copy. To make it the more dramatic, he calls Velasquez "a painter then almost forgotten,"
which seems injudicious, and the etched copies "works of a
light character," which seems generous. Beruete has other
game in view. He is out to show that through this attraction
toward Velasquez, Goya took his natural place in the stream
of Spanish painting.

And that is excessive. Goya certainly is in the great stream
of Spanish painting. But not through having seen the work
of Velasquez. On the contrary: he belongs to it far more
naturally than Velasquez does. He has what Elliot Paul calls
the beat, the *rubato*, which is the heat, blood and dust of
Spain. All Spain is in Goya's art. And no particular thanks
are due to Velasquez, of all people, for that. To think so is to
think that a man born and bred in Aragon, living most of his

life in Madrid, knowing the country as few other artists have ever known a country, from bullring to cathedral and from smugglers' cave to throne room, had to learn its expression from Philip IV's sedate laureate. They spoke the same idiom. The idiom was Spain's. Velasquez talked only the court version. Goya learned that last and liked it least.

Artists often comment sardonically on the tendency of critics to tell them dogmatically what their work is about. And to change a man's whole scale of values for him, gratuitously, saying, in effect: You may think you were painting this, but *I'll* tell you what you were really doing. Thus supernal symbolism is read into painted shadows, and what a painter intended as a pretty girl is labelled the anguish of a race.

Goya has had an enormous amount of attention of this sort. It still goes on, reminding one, at times, of some one's observation that in a learned essay Watts-Dunton offered "much posthumous advice to Shelley." So we may as well proceed. Few people will now deny that Goya's paintings for the Quinta del Sordo are greater than all his religious paintings put together. Their influence on the art of the nineteenth and the twentieth century has been profound. Yet in asserting that, one is in danger of agreeing with Goya, who in his own house painted precisely what he most wanted to see, and what he was most strongly moved to do.

It is different when one ventures to say that his drawings are finer than his more formal art. For in the same letter to Zapater saying that he was sending him the Velasquez set, Goya also mentioned, casually, that he was planning to send him some sketches, but Sabatini pounced on them. However, there was one he had about a dance, and Zapater was welcome to it if he wanted it. "As it was useless, it was left."

One hopes Zapater eventually got the sketch. In these casual drawings Goya miraculously put down the spirit and the movement and the look of his time. Some of the sketches of course are preliminary studies for works later carried out in paintings and murals and etchings. And many others are complete in their own existence—as the studies are—enough to make one see the genius of Goya. For here he was freest, without the necessities imposed by space, suitability and patrons in their several tyrannies.

6

GOYA's encounters with the lean old huntsman, Charles III, were sedate and few. The best of the Spanish Bourbons was almost as legendary in his own lifetime as he was to become in the history of a nation that has been inclined to honor him considerably above his value.

Islanded, as young Zapater remarked, Goya lived in Madrid until 1779, and in that year he had occasion to go to the palace and see the king for the first time in formal audience. The king, the heir apparent and Maria Luisa all praised his painting. So did the grandees around them. As he told Zapater, he couldn't have asked more cordial admiration, whether his work deserved it—and whether they were competent to judge it—or not. The royal enthusiasm was particularly useful since he was aware that he was drawing more implacable enemies as his prestige in painting rose.

He was ready to face the fact that the strong enemies were there. The enmity toward Goya was not based on what he had done wrong but on what he had done right: it increased in force and virulence in proportion to his success. For of course if Goya's work had been as bad as they said it was they would not have bothered to attack it. The better he got the more his enemies would say he was not a good artist. The more successful he was the more he would stir the rancorous to say his success was undeserved. The more he was paid the more they would say he was not worthy of his hire. And the more commissions he got from Church and Crown the more they would call him a revolutionary and an atheist.

Goya's way with critics was apt to be strenuous. By preference he would throw them downstairs. The joy we take in seeing the critic roasted and the satirist lampooned, is human. The theory that they shouldn't mind having done to them what they do to others is perhaps a shade idealistic. Carried to its logical conclusion it would have us believe that the hangman shouldn't mind being hanged.

Two tales from Stokes and Matheron may show how the blood of Aragon could boil: "Although Goya was a fierce critic, he objected to criticism. One critic who entered his studio had a large hat pushed over his head upon his shoulders. 'Learn to respect the head big enough to carry this hat' was the explanation. A second, asked to take a seat, was suddenly bespattered with paint, with the remark, 'I give you dirt for dirt. I disfigure you as you disfigure me.' Yet Goya remained on very good terms with Cean Bermudez—who was, perhaps, a better man than a critic."

Goya painted Charles III at his favorite occupation, in hunting costume. The king holds a gun like a staff in his hand. His face, the color of a wineskin, has a look of shrewd,

droopy sapience. There is a fat dog at his feet, wearing a
royal collar that always reminds me of Pope's

> *I am his highness' dog at Kew:*
> *Pray tell me sir, whose dog are you?*

The portrait of the king is probably not from life. It owes
something to Velasquez for the staging, and I have seen a
print after Mengs that suggests Goya paid him a compliment
for the likeness. One might find Beruete's observation that
Goya did not mention Charles III's posing for him the more
convincing if it were not for the fact that Goya doesn't mention painting a portrait of Charles III at all, in his letters to
Zapater. And when Beruete said that the head seemed to be
a copy of another work, "probably one of a different painter,"
he was apparently unaware of the Mengs. At any rate, the
portrait is decidedly by Goya.

It is the best remembered likeness of Isabel Farnese's son,
who came to the throne of Spain from a Naples he did not
particularly want to leave, with plans for making Spain into
the sort of country that it obviously had no bent for being.
What Charles III wanted to do to Spain was develop it for all
the world as though he had been commissioned to put it in
shape for Englishmen making the eighteenth-century Grand
Tour. In the manner of the time's benevolent despots, he was
always readier to give the country more law-enforcement
officers to put down smuggling than to see that the price of
commodities was fair enough to make smuggling unnecessary.
And to suppress riots rather than to see that land was distributed and taxation made less crushing: which would have
removed the cause of rioting.

Spain has always suffered from civil disorders. There is a popular theory that this is due to the fact that Spaniards are great individualists. The theory is poppycock. If Spaniards are individualists, so are the people of any other country under the sun. If they show it more it is because, in default of just governments, the individual has so often been forced to look to his own fists for survival. Civil disorder is a mark of desperation, not of exuberance.

To understand Goya's late-eighteenth-century Spain it is useful to know that its regalia was sumptuous and that the people went hungry to support the regalia. When Charles III went on his daily hunting expeditions it was on carefully fenced-off land worthy of a king. That land, of course, would have supported many hundreds of peasants who were under the necessity of trying to raise enough to live on from land so bleak the king did not have any use for it as hunting preserve.

This was the best of the Spanish Bourbons. Accustomed to the family's galloping incompetence, one is more ready to see the good in Charles III's pedestrian excellences. Compared with his ministers he seems to have had in him more than a fair share of the commonplace; compared with his successors, he seems to have had a touch of sheer genius.

If ever a monarch had the right to say: After me, the deluge, it was Charles III. He died the winter before the French Revolution began to flare across the Pyrenees. Yet before he died he had seen the new ideas of human liberty that were abroad coming into Spain. And he had done his best to smash them.

As Goya shows, his best was considerably more effective than his son's, and his son's sons, could be. Charles IV, who succeeded to the throne, was a fool. And the fool, Madariaga once remarked, was followed by the knave. That knave was Ferdinand VII, a man of such memorable ill-fame that in the days before the Republic was established the most insulting thing Spaniards could conceive as an epithet—in a land where the number of epithets is only exceeded by their wit—to call the king was to refer to him as Ferdinand Seven-and-a-Half.

Goya did not deal so mildly with ram-headed Charles IV and his contemptible son. He knew them. He knew them as thoroughly and unsparingly as an artist of genius has ever known men unworthy of the mildest power and yet in a position to decide the fate of millions from Bilbao to Buenos Aires. And their fate was in his hands. When Napoleon saw the raddled, bedevilled and horrible Queen Maria Luisa at Bayonne, he got an impression that he afterwards expressed by saying: "Her character is in her face, and it is incredible." Goya's judgment of the queen, her husband and her son is not less flattering. But it is credible.

It may be said, as Chapman and Altamira have said, that under Charles III Spain "reached the highest point she has attained since the sixteenth century" without unduly praising the state of affairs in the Spain Goya knew. But to add that Charles III "brought Spain forward to the position of a first-rank power again" is to be in danger of forgetting that other first-rank powers were well able to cope with that monarch's most astute policies.

For the truth is that in opposing England, Charles III got in the way of a machine powerful enough to plow on until the principal obstacle in her way—Napoleon—was destroyed. And in supporting the American colonies in their revolt—a guarded, mean, grudging support, as the story of John Jay's mission to Spain shows—Charles III helped establish a democratic principle that was eventually to wipe out Spain's own colonial power in the New World. It was only temporarily to his advantage to support the cause of American liberty; in the long view, it was absurd. His wars against England did him little good. The Bourbon Family Compact of 1761 tied him to the tails of the royal house of France, and that did him less good. In foreign affairs, where his abilities were tested by being matched against those of the world's foremost statesmen, his policies were in the end disastrous. In domestic matters, where the most modest efforts to do something for a plundered, valiant country were fought by the grandees and received incredulously by the people, his policies have won him a good deal of admiration.

He was usually on the side of French armies in war, but he was scarcely a follower of the French manner at court. In the palaces of Charles III life was ceremonious, stiff and gloomy. He liked hunting above all other occupations; the number of carefully brought up birds and rabbits that fell annually before his gun was prodigious. He was against dancing. He disapproved of the theatre. He objected to bullfighting so much that finally, in 1785, he abolished it, officially. That, of course, could not be permanent in Spain. Bullfighting returned, more popular than ever. Charles IV was inaugurated with a gala bullfight. And though from time to time bullfighting was abolished again, again it returned, always.

The Spanish people were remarkably fond of their kings

for the simple reason that they knew no other way of life, that veneration for the throne was drummed into them from the cradle to the grave, and that any opinions suggesting other methods of government were apt to be smashed out in blood. Yet Spaniards could draw the line at obeying their king's unreasonable demands. Charles III might frown—but dancing and the theatre went on in spite of his edicts.

And the first time he tried to stop Spaniards from wearing their cloaks up to their cheekbones and their hats down to their eyes the people rioted violently enough to overthrow the responsible minister, Squillace. Aranda, wiser, thought of a better plan. He simply issued a decree making the masking hat and cloak the official executioner's costume. Yet Goya's paintings for the tapestry cartoons show that the costume remained popular. It was characteristic of Goya to embody it in pictures meant to hang on the walls of one of the royal palaces.

Charles III was a devout Catholic, but he was also a devout believer in his own kingship. He consented to the expulsion of the Jesuits, and considerably reduced the power of the Inquisition. There was, of course, a general hostility toward the Jesuits in various parts of Europe. The Pope took notice of it, and when the expelled Jesuits tried to land at Civita Vecchia, Altamira relates, they were told by Cardinal Torrigiani to keep away or he would open fire on their boats.

The number of people in religious orders in Spain was somewhat reduced in Charles III's time. Chapman and Altamira note that in 1787—when Goya was forty-one years old —"on the basis of the usual size of Spanish families" there was approximately "one churchman to every five to ten adult men."[1]

The incorrigibly curious Casanova has left us this record of Charles III's day: "He dresses at seven, then goes into his dressing-room and has his hair done. At eight o'clock he says his prayers, then hears mass and, when this is over, takes chocolate and an enormous pinch of snuff, over which his big nose ruminates for some minutes; this is his only pinch in the whole day. At nine o'clock he sees his ministers and works with them till eleven. Then comes dinner, which he always takes alone, then a short visit to the Princess of the Asturias and at twelve sharp he gets into his carriage and drives to the hunting grounds. At seven he takes a morsel wherever he happens to be and at eight o'clock comes home so tired that he goes to sleep before he can get his clothes off. This keeps down the desires of the flesh."[2] It was Casanova's firm belief that Charles III died mad.

7

IN GOYA'S house there were always children. He had twenty sons and daughters. But in that day of large families the mortality was tragically high. There were too often occasions when the excitement over a new son, who would certainly grow up to be a painter like his father, or perhaps an illustrious torero, better than Pepe-Hillo or Pedro Romero, and who certainly had the look of robustious health, had scarcely begun before the child's life was over.

The *guapos muchachos* he wrote Zapater about from time to time seldom lived long after his exuberant announcement

[1] *A History of Spain,* p. 454.
[2] *The Memoirs of Jacques Casanova.* Translated by Arthur Machen.

of their arrival. What was the cause? All the evils of ignorant care and medieval methods. Only one son survived Goya, and no daughters. Yet a few lived on for months, and the midnight air of Madrid knew their voices raised in the piercing and mysterious night cries of infancy. In the daytime they would be all over the house, banging their heads on chairs, sweeping plates off tables, delightedly experimenting with their father's paints and brushes on canvases meant for portraits of the hidalgos and on walls not precisely intended for their murals.

Goya saw in their young efforts to draw traces of surprising talent more often than not, as other parents in other lands and other centuries have been known to do. And with not much more reward for what was, at root, hope and affection rather than discernment.

One child he particularly hoped would become an artist was his son Javier. When the *Caprichos* were given over into the king's hands a part of the bargain was that Javier should be given an annuity to study art. The one thing he asked in return for the plates and the sets of the *Caprichos* that had not been sold in the Street of Disenchantment in Madrid, he wrote Cayetano Soler, was "some recompense for my son Francisco Javier Goya so that he may be able to travel; he has the inclination and a great disposition to improve himself." And in his letter acknowledging the termination of the negotiations Goya wrote that he was very pleased at "the pension of twelve thousand *reales* that his majesty has conceded my son."[1]

---

[1] I hardly know how to give he whereabouts of Goya documents today. Goya's letter to Cayetano Soler used to be in the Palace archives in Madrid. It was written in July, 1803. The letter on the termination of the negotiations, written in October, 1803, was in the Prado. They are cited from Calleja.

Javier accomplished nothing spectacular with the annuity. The genius of his father was decidedly not in him. It is a wry commentary to think that the money given his son to travel abroad was based on the *Caprichos* that first made Goya famous in foreign countries. In the same letter to Cayetano Soler Goya said of the *Caprichos* when they first appeared in Madrid that *"los extranjeros son los que mas las desean"*—the foreigners are the ones who want them most. Indeed, travellers in Spain might well want to have sets of the *Caprichos* to take back with them as remembrances of their journey. For it is probable that they had heard tales of the profligate court and all its vices long before they went to Madrid. And they would be told various enough tales of the people the *Caprichos* lampooned. So that here was not only superb art but also an embodiment of the scandalous chronicle of Spain in that time. And it has been said that officers in Wellington's armies brought Goya's *Caprichos* back to England as trophies of their adventures in Spain.

Years after he had seen that his son Javier would never be an artist Goya again thought he had found a child who had the character for the severe and arduous discipline of art.

This time it was a girl. Idle speculation or a desire to pay Goya a compliment has made her his daughter. She was the young Rosario, daughter of Leocadia, who shared with Goya the near exile of the Quinta del Sordo and the far exile of Bordeaux.

Though Goya was sixty-eight when Rosario was born in Madrid in 1814, even the most scrupulous have at times called her Goya's "god-daughter" within significant quotation marks. It is apparent that she was a delightful child to have around; it is obvious that Goya adored her. Stokes, who has traced her history with unflagging interest, calls her "the most charming feature of his residence in Bordeaux." When Rosario was ten, Goya, who had been experimenting again in drawing very small pictures through a magnifying glass, wanted her to be taught miniature painting.

He wrote Ferrer: "This astonishing child wishes to learn miniature painting and I wish it also, for to paint as she is painting at her age is the greatest phenomenon in the world. She possesses special qualities, as you will see. If you will be good enough to help me I want to send her to Paris, but I would like you to consider her as if she were my daughter. I will repay you with my works, or my goods. I send you a small sample of her ability. All the professors at Madrid have marvelled at it, particularly the incomparable Martin."

Goya's devotion to Rosario is superbly shown in his offer to repay Ferrer with his works or his goods; his reference to "my daughter" has occasioned more conclusions than the plain words require. His hope that she might study in Paris was not fulfilled, and his boundless faith in her qualities was more than she had the capacity to carry out. All that Goya and the art schools of Bordeaux could teach her she learned. But she could not be taught enough to follow Goya. After he died she went back to Spain. Stokes has found that she became an accomplished copyist in the Prado. She became, in the descending scale, drawing teacher to Queen Isabella. Her life was not long. At twenty-six she died of the shock of a riot in Madrid. And if she disappointed Goya as Javier had disappointed him long ago, she at least gave him brightness and gayety.

8

IN 1780 Goya plunged into a variety of activities that on the whole were rather less tranquil than the painting of tapestry cartoons. Indeed, he was not to go back to the scenes for tapestries for half a dozen years.

It was in this year that he went up to Zaragoza to do the murals for the Cathedral of Pilar. The paintings were intended to be sacred; the rows over them that Goya got into were decidedly profane.

But with another painting that was sacred and that was also a part of the work of that year he had more success. This was a painting of the Crucifixion he presented to the Academy of San Fernando in Madrid on the occasion of his becoming a member of that influential citadel of Spanish art. If it is true that few artists were ever less suited to the rôle of academician than Goya it must be said that few of his paintings were ever more completely academic than the Crucifixion he painted for the Academy. It is lifeless and without conviction.

The most striking description of that painting you will find is in Ernest Hemingway's *Death in the Afternoon:* "Goya's crucifixion is a cynically romantic, wooden oleograph that could serve as a poster for the announcement of crucifixions in the manner of bullfight posters. A crucifixion of six carefully selected Christs will take place at five o'clock in the Monumental Golgotha of Madrid, government permission having been obtained. The following well-known, accredited and notable crucifiers will officiate, each accompanied by his cuadrilla of nailers, hammerers, cross-raisers and spade men, etc."

Goya's heart was not in that work in that time. For as Hemingway goes on to remark, Goya believed "in blacks and in grays, in dust and in light, in high places rising from the plains, in the country around Madrid, in movement, in his own cojones, in painting, in etching, and in what he had seen, felt, touched, handled, smelled, enjoyed, drunk, mounted, suffered, spewed-up, lain with, suspected, observed, loved, hated, lusted, feared, detested, admired, loathed, and destroyed. Naturally no painter has been able to paint all that but he tried."

Later on, when Goya was in a rare pious mood toward the end of his life, he did paint a true Christ. It is the *Oración*. It used to be very hard to see the *Oración*. It was in the school side of San Antón, down behind the Puerta del Sol in one of those bent streets where you are apt to get a Sevillano with your change. The Father at the door didn't think they had any such painting, he thought you must mean the one in the church next door. But since you had come all the way from Norte America to see it—had your government sent you, and was English the common language of Norte America?—he was very polite about it, and, though it was getting pretty dark and there seemed to be no intention of turning on too many lights, you might follow him.

You went through the high inner doors then, and upstairs away from the church side, into the school part, where, on the court, a Father of higher rank joined you, and you were shown the side where the charity pupils studied, and the side where the others dedicated to the priesthood stayed.

All the way you saw paintings. On the roof of the stair well there was a mural, on the walls many paintings, badly framed, battered and neglected and a great hodgepodge of good and bad. No Goyas there. You kept getting deeper into the walls of the priestly labyrinth. Semi-Grecos and Murillo-ish stuff on the corridor walls. What size was the Goya? You said it could be large or small. That seemed a surprise. Well, finally, the one with the bun-pinched hat and the pompon led the way into the large inner room, his office and bedroom, where brown-striped pajamas lay on the turned-down iron bed, and you looked around at the paintings on the walls, a good many of them.

And on the inner wall facing the window, high up and not two feet tall, was Goya's painting, the figure kneeling with arms outstretched, looking up at the beam of light and the cup, simple and swiftly painted and true, discolored now, and dark, yet lit by the smoky white color. You took it down from the wall and looked at the date; it was either 1815 or 1819, but more likely 1819, the year when Goya was very close to death.

He was far from death in 1780 when he painted the *Crucifixion* for the Royal Academy of San Fernando.

Goya presented the painting on the fifth of July, and two days later he became a member of San Fernando. Years later the painting was taken to the Prado, where it hung among his masterpieces as the most unanswerable affirmation of the fact that Goya was never meant to be a pious master of religious art.

"For my house I don't need much in the way of belongings," Goya wrote Zapater. "With a print of Nuestra Señora del Pilar, a table, five chairs, a frying pan, a wineskin, a guitar, a roasting jack and a lamp, everything else is unnecessary."

He was getting ready to go to Zaragoza. And that letter was written May 10, some five months before he started north.

La Pepa was in her customary state: pregnant. August 9 Goya wrote: "My wife thanks you very much, and she wants me to tell you that the home is woman's tomb, she thinks the place sad, but I repeat to you that if you know it's the case, you'll carry it out."

"La Pepa has already given birth," he wrote two weeks later, "thank God a very healthy boy. With which we'll arrive sooner than I had thought."

Those battles over the frescoes for Pilar in Zaragoza were enormously significant in Goya's life. They brought the rivalry between Goya and his brother-in-law, the singularly competent and thoroughly mediocre painter Francisco Bayeu, into the open. And I do not think it would be injudicious to ascribe some of Goya's less orthodox views of the clergy to this conflict with ecclesiastical authority.

What happened? Goya, as we know, had already done some painting in the dim upper reaches of Pilar during the 1770's. There was much more decoration needed, and Bayeu —Francisco, the elder, not young Ramón, who was Goya's age and his companion in painting cartoons for the tapestries that were to adorn the palaces—was in charge of it. And from the beginning, Goya did not like that. It is obvious that he had a generous amount of scorn for his brother-in-law's abilities. But Goya's rows were not all with Bayeu; the authorities in charge of Pilar caught a full measure of his anger.

Ramón worked with Goya at Pilar. Francisco worked against him. It was the old division all over again. Yet the preliminaries were mild enough. Indeed, when Goya's sketches were presented to the authorities in the autumn of 1780 the members of the committee liked them very much; they went, so far as to commend Goya's taste. But it was not a lasting mood of serenity. By December Francisco Bayeu had arrived on the scene, and then the wars began.

If you could go into Pilar Cathedral in Zaragoza today and look at those frescoes you might wonder whether they were ever worth so much rancorous fury. Certainly they are uninspired enough, from any point of view. If Bayeu had complained that they were dull he might have been on firm ground; instead he seemed to think that they were dangerously unorthodox in style. The true root of the difficulty, apparently, was not in the painting at all. It was in the fact that Bayeu tried to give Goya orders, that Goya resented being told how to paint by Bayeu, and that Goya said so with considerable vehemence.

Bayeu then asked, somewhat sulkily, to be excused from having anything more to do with Goya's painting. This did not please the authorities at all. They had put the work in Bayeu's charge; Bayeu had brought Goya to paint with him; why couldn't they get along? Still, after a good deal of discussion, they decided to delegate the perilous responsibility of overseeing Goya to Canon Allué, who was also to go to Goya as a friend and persuade him to be more mild in his attitude toward Bayeu.

Canon Allué did what he could. But it was not enough. For no sooner had Goya completed the dome than every one began to complain about it. The coached people of Zaragoza were persuaded to say that they preferred the trite painting of Bayeu to the more vigorous and more modern work of Goya. And in February, 1781, when Goya submitted his designs for the decoration of the triangles in the side arches, the authorities said his figures representing Faith, Courage, Charity and Patience—of all inappropriate subjects at that moment—were indecent.

9

THERE was not, they said, enough drapery on Goya's goddesses. The authorities were in another uproar, while Goya, waiting, grew shorter in temper by the minute. When Canon Allué was sent to ask Bayeu to take charge again, and see that Goya used less dark color and more raiment on his goddesses, Bayeu, as Calvert remarks, retaliated with a tirade on his injured dignity.

And when Allué went to ask Goya to make peace with his brother-in-law, Goya sent the authorities a reply that is at once a masterpiece of rebuttal and an extraordinarily revealing insight into his character. I quote it here[1] in Calvert's excellent translation, though I am convinced that a lawyer, rather than Goya, drew up the document:

"D. Francisco de Goya, Member of the Royal Academy of San Fernando, respectfully shows: That after having put the works of his profession before the public, namely, the

[1] *Goya, An Account of His Life and Works.* By Albert F. Calvert. London: John Lane, The Bodley Head. 1908.

paintings just unveiled at the Church of Our Lady of Pilar, his attention has been called to the opinions he hears expressed, containing a criticism prompted by a principle other than that of justice, or governed by the authorised rules of art, which only should form the opinion regarding the work; and although he cannot believe that ill-meant prejudice has gained access to your rectitude, or that you could be led away by impulses little in accord with reason; yet the honour of a professor is a very delicate thing; opinion is what sustains him, his subsistence depends on his reputation, and when that is obscured by even a light shadow, his fortune is gone; therefore Nature warns him to take care of it by using all the defences within his reach, and to omit the least would be to gain a slight advantage by abandoning the greatest treasure the Creator has entrusted to him.

"These principles, accompanied by a sense of wounded honour, the expositor hopes his explanation will make evident to your benignity.

"D. Francisco Bayeu asked that the work in the domes might be done by his brother and the expositor, but it was on the understanding that the latter should do one of the parts by himself, as Bayeu himself agreed, considering that the degree of an honoured member of the San Fernando Academy, acquired by the work which had won great renown for him in Madrid, in addition to the work for H.M., would not admit of his absolute subordination to another professor without detriment to his honour."

There Goya himself blazes out through the smoky haze of formal wordage; there is the heart of the matter. He is damned if he will have Bayeu or any one else tell him how to paint.

He goes on to say that he may be wrong in thinking so, but he believes Bayeu himself—as well as Allué—would agree with him.

Goya then reminded the authorities at Pilar that they had approved his first designs, that he had consulted Bayeu, that he had wanted to work in harmony with his brother-in-law. But he goes back to his main contention when he says there are those who pretended, when the work was under way, that "the agreement with Bayeu was that he [Bayeu] should interfere as much as he liked with the expositor's [Goya's] work, and that the latter should obey him as a subordinate in execution, placing of figures, style, coloring and so forth; in a word make him a mere executor and mercenary subordinate; but as this was in direct opposition to what had been agreed, it would have been discreditable to his honour to yield, as he would be losing what his merit had won for him, and he could not therefore so humiliate himself, for he knew that the previous offices were sufficient, and that similar ones if continued would not make them anything but his own production."

Ironically enough, the tables were turned, many years after both Goya and Bayeu were dead, when a painting by Bayeu[1] was hung in the Prado under the impression—which even Beruete shared—that it had been painted by Goya.

As for Bayeu's saying he would no longer be responsible for Goya's work, that, Goya told the authorities, was to create lack of confidence in him. Goya then went on to speak of the rumors circulated against him, accusing him (certainly not for the last time!) of "hauteur, pride and stubbornness."

[1]Feliciana Bayeu, niece of Goya, and a very pretty girl, too.

After that, he said, the plan of creating personal antagonism as a prelude to public criticism of his work was complete.

In truth, Goya was thoroughly tired of Bayeu's way of trying to block him at every turn. Exasperated with his brother-in-law's habit of saying a design was good one day and bad another, he told the authorities plainly that he was through.

He had heard that alterations were to be made in his work. If that were true, Goya suggested, the authorities might save themselves some terrible future embarrassment by having competent artists look at his work before any dauber—a clear enough allusion to Bayeu—marred it. He suggested Maella or Antonio Velasquez, and he offered to pay their expenses from Madrid. And with that parting reflection for Bayeu, Allué and the authorities of Pilar to brood on, Goya signed his communication on the seventeenth of March, 1781.

For a time after that there was a distinct threat of peace in Zaragoza. Inflammatory though the letter was, it had given Goya a chance to blow off steam completely. When, as Viñaza has shown, Allué got Goya's old friend Father Salzedo to go and ask Goya to take a less martial and more charitable attitude toward Bayeu, Goya, surprisingly enough, said he would. New sketches were prepared by Goya—presumably putting more clothing on the bodies of the goddesses.

But there was too much lightning in the air. And in May the final storm broke. Once more Goya and Bayeu were embattled over the way the painting was being done—had the draperies come off the goddesses again?—and the authorities faced Goya's fury. This time there was no compromise. The authorities decided that Goya was too rebellious to have around. The committee decided to ask Goya to stop painting in Pilar—and, like other building custodians more than a century later—have the space covered by a more docile hand. Goya, as Viñaza has found in the old records of Zaragoza, told Allué that he was only jeopardizing his reputation there. He said a furious farewell to Zaragoza, and returned to Madrid.

The last touch of rancor came when the ecclesiastical authorities in Zaragoza announced that they were giving decorations to Josefa, on the ground that she was the sister of their own Francisco Bayeu, and none to Goya.

10

THE Cross opposed him. He went to the Crown for vindication, and he got it. The indignation over the way he had been annoyed at Zaragoza was balanced; it was not forgotten; it rankled for years.

He wrote Zapater on the 25th of July, 1781, telling him what was in the wind. The greatest opportunity in painting that has ever been offered in Madrid, he said—not without enormous exaggeration—was soon to be undertaken at the direction of the king. His majesty had decided to hold a competition for paintings for the Church of San Francisco el Grande (a large church that Charles IV was bent upon making into a kind of national pantheon) and Goya was named as one of the competing painters.

Goya was triumphant. He told Zapater to tell the news around in Zaragoza, that it might come to the ear of those who had shown such a singular lack of appreciation toward him there. Bayeu—the great Bayeu himself—was to be one of the competing painters. Not to mention Maella and the rest of the court painters. That Goya had been chosen was something he hoped would properly impress the sinverguenzas in Zaragoza who had failed to appreciate his merit. The size of the painting was to be nine Spanish yards by four and a half. And Goya knew that Zapater would be able in his behalf to strike some telling blows with that news.

Still furious over the Zaragozan wars, he devoted himself to the painting for San Francisco with an ardor he might ordinarily seldom feel for a commission in religious art. His letters to Zapater in Zaragoza are peppered with references to it. He was working on the sketch for his painting. He noted what progress he was making. He kept bringing it up over and over again, showing how much it meant to him, how anxious he was to make a success of it.

In these years Goya had various family troubles interspersed with troubles of his own devising.

Goya wrote a moving letter to Zapater November 13, 1781, after hearing that Zapater's sister had died, and knowing that his own father had not long to live.

"Martin mío," Goya wrote. "I have heard with deep feeling the notice about the sister and I have commended her to God; but the belief I have has consoled me that she was muy buena and she has gained a good piece of glory, which we, who have been so tunantes (dissolute) need to mend our ways in the time we have left. [Goya had 47 years left to live.] You are not at a loss ever for ideas, and I am not clever at writing, for I consider myself far below your superior talent. I am also expecting the sad news that my father will die one day soon, since they write me that there is little hope, and the doctor, who is Ortiz, also has written me: I have only the regret that I cannot be there to have this consolation. For Camillo I am hoping that he will go to Toledo to see whether God wills that he may be a curate and if he doesn't we will think of anything else here so he'll get something."

In truth, Goya was a little stale. He had forced himself to achieve an earnestness that was not natural. His work showed it. What was worse, he felt it. He was thoroughly tired of painting—at least of that double drudgery. In exasperation he wrote Zapater: "Pray to the Virgin"—the Virgin of Pilar, who is the patroness of all men of Aragon, so much so that even the Anarchists have seen distinct signs of admiration for their cause in her—"pray to the Virgin to give me more desire to work." Since he liked above all the hunting which he talked about constantly in his letters, always noting whether he had been or not, and what luck he had, he wished he were in Zaragoza, so that he could see his old friend, "take nothing from nobody, and go out hunting every day."

Goya's father was soon dead. Viñaza found the record in Zaragoza, and Beruete quotes it with the famous last line: "José Goya, husband of Engracia Lucientes, died on the 17 December 1781, and was buried in the principal nave of San Miguel. *No testó porque no tenía de que.*" In September, 1783, Goya brought his mother down to Madrid. But she did not like life there. Or she may not have enjoyed life in Goya's turbulent household, and she went back to Zaragoza in 1784.

Camillo, one of Goya's brothers, the one who had become a priest, also turned up in Madrid and took up the chaplaincy at Chinchón, through the influence of Don Luis. And this further stirred the ferocity of Goya's enemies. Camillo wrote Zapater: "I didn't write you as soon as I got here because I couldn't give you the sort of news I'd like to about Francho." That was Goya. "For he, although God has given him good fortune and ability, they have persecuted him with such force that since they can't tarnish his accomplishments (for this isn't Zaragoza) they destroy patience if he has said something or if he has not said anything, and reversing with their lying all they possibly can, so that in the hour I write you I am sick at heart. And since things are so, I can't say what I want to say. The worst part of it is that they make him loathe painting, and since they are not able to make him lose his talent they try to make him not want to go on painting, or at least he is exposed to that. For they can't stand seeing him praised so much and honored so highly above all the rest. So I hope you'll forgive me, and see that I can't write Don Juan Martin"—that was Goicoechea, the rich merchant of Zaragoza who was a patron of the artistic renaissance up there.

II

AND wider horizons opened in 1783. In that year he had two enormously profitable commissions: to paint Floridablanca (which yielded profit in prestige rather than money, as he indignantly observed) and to paint the family of the king's romantic brother, Don Luis, who had married a lady not of royal rank, and so suffered the treatment from authority that still might be observed in other countries some time later.

He had yet, as Beruete points out, to form a style; though he was nearly thirty-seven and was to be one of the greatest portrait painters the world has known, he had not yet done anything memorable. The awful influence of his training under the estimable Luzan, the despotic Mengs and the jealous Bayeu were in all he had done so far.

In January he wrote Zapater about the Floridablanca portrait, and in September about his entertaining stay at Don Luis's country house.

Floridablanca, a man of brilliant eminence, was minister to the king and author of some of the best reforms of the age. Goya had known him for some time; indeed he wrote Zapater with a touch of inconsequence, "I owe so much to this gentleman that this afternoon I have been with his señora for two hours after her dinner, for she has come in to dine in Madrid."

It was Floridablanca, the Floridablanca of Goya's astonishing portrait, who tried, during the first years of Charles IV's reign—before Godoy, the Queen's favorite, supplanted him—to shore up the crumbling structure of Royal sovereignty. At first he attempted to carry on the moderately humane reforms of Charles III.

But the new ideas in France cooled the heart of Floridablanca. He favored benevolence toward the people, but not freedom; it upset him to find that there was a growing tendency abroad for them to take as their right what he would not even concede as a possible gift from a kindly sovereign and his ministers.

Floridablanca was a part of the old order that was dying in Spain—how often has that old order died?—and he was determined to save the throne at a time when, as the turn of the wheel was soon to show, he could not even save himself. He, who was able to think he might help to stop the French Revolution in its course, was easily convinced that he could prevent its ideas from entering Spain.

His measures were merciless. In April, 1791, he published a decree suppressing all newspapers in Spain with the exception of the Official Gazette. "Strict watch was kept on the frontier to prevent the passage of news or propaganda from France," Hume observed, and in the summer "a monstrous decree was published which brought upon Spain the protests of all Europe. Every foreigner in Spain, resident or traveller"—and Hume points out significantly that half of them were Frenchmen—"was to swear allegiance to the King of Spain and the Catholic religion, and renounce all claim or right of appeal for protection to his own nationality, under the most atrocious penalties. Whilst, on the one hand, he was showing his fear of the French Revolution, and refusing to recognize the sovereignty of the people proclaimed by the Assembly (July, 1789), Floridablanca was, on the other, appealing to the family compact [between those strange victims of technological unemployment, the Bourbons] to claim armed French aid against England in support of Spain's pretension to the possession of the whole of the west coast of North America." There he went too far—he was both trying to destroy the French Revolution and to get the revolutionists (who seemed surprisingly willing) to help him against England. Only a swift negotiation between the English ambassador and Charles IV avoided the start of another war with England then and there.

A PAINTER FROM ARAGON

It was only a postponement of war with England, in any case. One has merely to say Trafalgar to remember that peace with England, in that epoch, was rarer than war.

Floridablanca was removed from office in the Autumn of 1792, however; and Aranda, who for a time professed to admire the French Revolution, took his place. The repressive measures of Floridablanca were loosened. But Aranda was not destined for long tenure. The queen had set her heart on making the guardsman of destiny, Godoy, premier; and, as usual, she soon had her way. Floridablanca was still in his liberal phase when he was being painted by Goya.

He worked at that portrait with prodigious energy: "To-day I have put in the head of the portrait for.Señor Moñino" —that was Floridablanca's name before Charles III ennobled him—"in his presence and have succeeded in getting a good likeness and he is very pleased." He worked on. The head certainly was all that the most patient sitter in Spain would wait for at one sitting; a dozen tubes were squeezed to fill other details. On and on he painted, for all the world as though he had the last stretched canvas available, and the history of Floridablanca must be preserved without abridgment there. And finally it was completed. The result pleased Floridablanca, and, to be fair, it must be admitted that it pleased others. It is, one feels, a tribute to the recognition of honest toil, not the admiration of art, that inspires such judgments.

For Goya's portrait of Floridablanca is one of the most revealing of his early pictures. All that Goya had learned from Mengs and Bayeu that is meretricious is collected in it;

the full force of eighteenth-century pretentiousness is gathered there.

To enumerate the contents of that painting is an inventory; to remember half of them, a feat of memory.

Floridablanca dominates the scene, and in succeeding in doing so he gives an account of his force that is impressive. He stands, wigged and medalled in knee-breeches in a complicated posture: taking a step forward with his left foot, the right foot soundly planted on the rug, the left arm bent and the right one pointing eyeglasses to the left. He himself looks straight ahead, as though toward footlights. The reason the right hand extends is because Goya has painted himself in at full length there, holding up a canvas, and the eyeglasses are deputies of interest.

And in case any one should not recognize the man holding the canvas up for inspection or dream who it might possibly be, a paper lies at his feet labelled: "Señor Fco. Goya." Another man looks over Floridablanca's left shoulder, probably Floridablanca's secretary; a portrait of the king hangs on the wall beyond, a book on the floor says: "Palomino—Practica de la Pintura, 2 y 3," a plan of the Canal of Aragon (one of Floridablanca's principal interests) lies on a table at the right, and on that table stands a huge and ornate clock. The light improves on nature; it comes from a cavernous opening in the draperies behind Goya, somehow refracts to shed a full radiance on Floridablanca, illuminates clock and plans and king, and picks out the more significant books and papers that strew the floor.

Goya would have got ahead faster if he had consulted the others. He scorned their connivings and their trades. Meantime, his way was rough and his advancement slow. He wrote Zapater in a black humor: "Amigo, there's no news. And so far there is more silence so far as my relations with Señor Moñino goes than before I painted his portrait. He said more when he looked at it and liked the portrait: 'Goya, we shall see about it by and by.' Every one is astonished that there has been no result whatever from the Minister of State after it had given him such pleasure, with the result that if there's nothing here there's nothing to hope for, and having had such high hopes the disappointment is so much the more."

"I'm feeling low" (estoy flaco), he wrote a little later on, "and I'm not doing much work: I haven't even finished the painting of the Infante on horseback, but it doesn't lack much. As for San Francisco, they're going to unveil the paintings for the Church; there'll be a good deal of tumult, for from now on we'll see how we come out there."

12

Goya and the Infante Don Luis were great friends. That romantic prince had been banished from court. He lived the life of a country gentleman and patron of the arts at Arenas de San Pedro, outside Madrid. Like his brother, Charles III, Don Luis was fond of hunting. He considered himself a good shot, and he was astonished to find that Goya was a better one. One may suspect that the courtiers surrounding Don Luis would not presume to bag more than their patron. No such consideration would ever bother Goya. He would not deliberately miss a bird for any one.

In the late summer of 1783 Goya spent some time at the

house of Don Luis. When he got·back to Madrid toward the end of September he wrote Zapater that the Infante was not a poor shot himself, that he had been given a thousand reales for his work and a gold and silver gown of considerable value for his wife, and that they had not been willing to let him go until he promised to return to Arenas every year. It may be that Don Luis, who was very pleased with the way Goya had painted the family, and who found him an entertaining companion, wanted to attach him to the household.

The astonishing swiftness with which Goya could paint a portrait when he wanted to is brought out in some notes Beruete has preserved about Goya's work at Arenas. A picture of the Infante's wife, Doña Maria Teresa de Villabriga, is marked as having been painted by Goya "between eleven and twelve on the morning of August 27, 1783." He did a portrait of Don Luis himself "between nine and twelve on the morning of September 11, 1783." That took, as you see, three times as long. Perhaps after that the sun came out, and they went hunting.

A child Goya painted on that visit to Arenas had a tragic life before her. She was the Infante's eldest daughter, Maria Teresa, known to history as the Countess of Chinchón, forced to marry Godoy so that the queen's lover should become a relative of the blood royal. Years later Goya painted another portrait of her, a somehow deeply sympathetic painting that makes you feel she is sad and lonely and lost.

The Infante was an unconventional man. His marriage to the beautiful lady from Aragon was not his first departure from general custom. At the age of eight he had been made a cardinal, but he decided early that he would not pursue a

San Fernando, Madrid

THE MAJAS ON THE BALCONY

religious career. In all truth, there was not much farther
that he could pursue it.

13

GOYA's paintings for the Osunas began in 1782 and went
on for a number of years. He visited their house—near Madrid—and there he painted and enjoyed himself as part of a
rather Edwardian court group. The blood of the Borgias ran
in the veins of the Duchess of Osuna. She was called the
proudest woman in Spain—though not, one imagines, when
the Duchess of Alba was there.

Lady Holland spoke well of the Duchess of Osuna, calling
her "the most distinguished woman in Madrid for her talents, worth and taste. She has acquired a relish for French
luxuries," Lady Holland noted, "without diminishing her
national magnificence and hospitality. She is very lively, and
her natural wit covers her total want of refinement and ac-
quirement. Her figure is very light and airy. She was formerly the great rival of the celebrated Dss. of Alba in
profligacy and profusion. Her *cortejo*, Peña, has been attached
for many years, and is now the only one established. She is
rather imperious in her family. Her revenues are greater even
than the D. of Osuna's, who is a very tolerably sensible man
and of considerable knowledge. He had great projects of
ambition, and acquired at the beginning of the French Revolution the surname of being another Orléans. He obtained
permission during his favor at Court to import from foreign
countrys what books he chose for his own library, notwithstanding they were prohibited by the Inquisition, and he
took advantage of this to collect a very good and extensive

library, chiefly of classics, history, voyages, and books of science, which he intended for the use of the public, but this intention he was not permitted by the Governt. to carry into effect. He has, after the Medinacelli, the greatest estate, but the Infantado is the most unincumbered at present."[1]

The Osunas lived in considerable splendor. They were festooned with titles, gathered through generations of intermarriage between the leading families of Spain. With each marriage new lands and palaces were collected to the family fold. One of their favorite places was the Alameda, to the south of Madrid. Goya painted many portraits for the family. One, a family group, is an incredibly stilted composition that may be taken as a satire on their way of life. The figures are bloodless, even the child playing with his toy coach in the foreground looks as though he were made of china.

The Duchess of Osuna was a woman of discernment in art. At court she was more popular with the nobility than with the queen. The Osunas bought many paintings from others. When the descendants of the family sold them in the nineties they went all over the world.

Goya's painting called *The Madhouse* belonged to the Osunas. It is an extraordinarily vivid picture. The insane are flung together in one vaulted dungeon. Some are naked. Some have dressed themselves in feathers and absurd clothes. Some are morose and hopeless, some are screaming with lunatic energy.

14

GOYA's huge painting of St. Bernard in San Francisco el Grande meant considerably more to his prestige in eigh-

[1]*The Spanish Journal of Elizabeth Lady Holland.* Edited by the Earl of Ilchester. Longmans, Green & Co. 1910.

teenth-century Madrid than it has meant to his timeless reputation as an artist.

There is St. Bernard, standing on a rock, a star above his
head like the star on a Christmas fir. An appreciative king
of Goya's own Aragon is looking up at the saint from the
foot of the stone, and various cloaked gallants—one with
the face of Goya—are around him. The saint's arms are outstretched; he is silhouetted against a fort's ramparts and a
great tree that is useful to the composition.

It is triumphant, it is Aragonese, it is Goya. And it is
neither very religious nor very moving. But it is a fine
decoration for a church wall. It was the finest picture that
any of the artists in that long and arduous competition produced. When it was shown it was apparent to all that Goya
had done better than the leading Spanish painters of his day.
He had vindicated his reputation after the infuriating quar-
rels in Zaragoza. He had established himself in Madrid.

Finally, in November, 1784, the great unveiling took
place. Goya wrote to Zapater triumphantly:

"They've been uncovered, all of them, and I don't want to
tell you more than that talking about them has begun and
a good deal of it, and it will be much better for you to hear
first from others the Justice that is done, for even the King is
going," and he goes on to recall a time when Zapater got
others to say for him what he might say.

All in all, he was feeling enormously happy. In December
he wrote on the 4th: "At present we're in the excitement of
the paintings of San Francisco, and always thanks to God the
comments go on as they began. Wednesday the King's going,
and I'll tell you what happens." On the 11th he told his

friend: "It's certain that I've had good fortune in the opinion of the authorities and the whole public with the painting at San Francisco, for they are all in my favor without any dispute, though up to now nothing has happened that should from above; we'll see what happens when the King returns and I'll let you know."

15

YET FOR all his religious experiences, Goya, in that same year, had some other successes. He painted two pictures for the Infante Don Luis and got 30,000 reales for them, and four paintings of saints in life-size for the College of Calatrava at Salamanca, which won him the thanks of the administration as a compliment to his painting, 400 doubloons for pay and expenses, and a letter of commendation from Jovellanos addressing him as Sr. Don Francisco *de* Goya, which confirmed his ideas on signing his name from then on.

And his wife gave birth to their annual son, which Goya mentioned in one of the letters—December 4—to Zapater: "The second of this month my wife gave light [dio luz] to a boy, very healthy and robust. He was baptized yesterday with the names of Francisco Pedro. The birth went off without trouble. I hope to God this can be successful."

He was in a mood to buy a carriage. The solemn competition had been very satisfactory: An extraordinarily dull painting had triumphed over six other canvases with even slighter claims to stir the heart or the mind of any man or girl who looked at them. In all truth, all one could say for it was that the ablest of seven mediocrities had carried the palm. If Goya had left us only such bathos as this we should be well served in hearing that he was only one painter in one of the most dismal periods of Spain's art. The academic was victorious. Certainly it gave no hope of the genius slowly maturing from a mind perfectly fitted to guide brushes that were to stab open the days of wrath ahead.

Yet it was tremendously important in the life of the man. Now he could look forward with some certitude to the prospect of having more work to do. For he had, in that one painting, pleased church and court. And these were the main sources of an artist's bread and butter in that time.

It was not much more than hope, so far. He wrote Zapater in the middle of January, 1785: "About my work there is nothing from above, nor do I suppose there will be, though I haven't been able to desire more than what has happened in the competition of San Francisco."

He soon had a lively hope of specific advancement. In March, 1785, he wrote Zapater that he had seen the royal family, and had talked to Don Luis, who was pretty ill and not expected to recover.

By May he was writing Zapater every few days. His letters of the 10th, 14th and 17th are practically diary entries. "In confidence: On Sunday the Academy considered naming me for the post of assistant director that was left vacant by the death of Calleja." The king, however, had to be consulted first. "The Academy post is the same Bayeu has. It only pays 25 doubloons a year—the Directorship 50—." And: "The King has sent down the approbation of the Directorship."

August brought the usual domestic news. He wrote Zapater a worried letter about his wife's illness, which, he suspected, was due to a miscarriage.

Apropos of this letter, young Zapater points his moral and adorns his tale of Goya's rectitude. Based on the letters Goya wrote the friend in Zaragoza, he says flatly that Goya was not the hellion Matheron and Iriarte said he was. He speaks feelingly of the "sacred obligations" of domesticity Goya fulfilled from 1777, when he was already married, on. Goya talked of domestic details constantly—at least in those letters, he did.

This much young Zapater will obliquely grant: "Thus there is no reason to say that the eccentric and singular character he manifested as artist and as man caused him to ignore to the point of culpability, the duties which, as husband and as father, he was obliged to fulfill, nor to say assuredly that Goya, by declaring himself free, never savored again the pleasures of conjugal life."

Zapater somewhat inconclusively points out that Goya's letters to his uncle are full of talk about how to invest his savings. (The Bank of Spain had, over a century later, one amazing record of that: "As a matter of fact, the Banco de España still keeps fifteen shares of stock to which the painter subscribed," Beruete wrote. These shares Goya had endorsed over to others in the late winter of 1788, possibly to raise money to buy one of his ineffable carriages.) He speaks of the money Goya sent his father and mother, and of things Goya bought for his wife, his brother Tomás and his sister Rita. All this is to show that Goya was a devoted husband, brother and son. He was, too. But that did not take all his energy by any means.

Goya was always, in fact, to the end of his life, fairly careful about his investments. Cean Bermudez, the critic and friend of Goya, was the man who advised him to invest in shares of the Bank of Spain.

In March, 1786, Goya wrote Zapater: "I have not what you have, for in all my work, with shares in the Bank and the Academy, I have not more than two or three thousand reales a year, and with this I'm as content as the most fortunate."

Still, he had more commissions always to look forward to, and he was learning to execute them with considerably more rapidity and assurance—and better art.

He bought the carriage. And, as he wrote Zapater a little ruefully, though with a certain pride, the first thing he did was to overturn it. He came out of the adventure temporarily lame in the right leg, and full of words. The carriage was very handsome, a barouche in the English manner—"*a la ynglesa*," and one of only three of its kind in Madrid. Why, he remarked, people in the streets stopped to stare at it. Well, the day he went out to try it, and the horse he'd bought to go with it, a ten-year-old, the man who was selling it to him was there. Goya had the reins, and they were bowling along at a gallop. The man asked Goya if he wanted to see how the Neapolitans turned. The man was a Neapolitan himself. Goya said yes he did; as he wrote Zapater, he always wanted to learn something new. So he gave the man the reins. And that was disastrous. The road was wide, but not wide enough for such goings on. The carriage not only turned around, but it turned over as well, sending barouche, horse, Goya and the man from Naples over into the ditch. Well, Goya said philosophically, it wasn't so bad, he had just been laid up since St. James's day, and he was expecting his doctor any minute now to tell him whether he could start walking again.

Otherwise, his affairs were in fair order. He had already established himself in an enviable way of life. Now he waited in no one's anterooms. Whoever wanted anything from him came to him. He had made himself desired. And if the person wasn't some one of considerable importance, or an old friend, he would not paint him. He worked for no man he didn't like.

The result was, of course, that he began to be sought out. People who wanted him to paint them came flocking to his house. And they wouldn't let him alone. He didn't know how he was going to fulfill all his commissions.

He told Zapater he couldn't do a Carmen for him because he was so busy with orders for the King. Those were probably the tapestry cartoons. But he had time to send Zapater some sausages and he thanked Zapater for some almond paste from Zaragoza, which was better than any he could get in Madrid.

16

DURING 1787 and 1788—the last years of Charles III's reign, as Zapater points out, and the stormy threshold of the French Revolution, as he does not—Goya, pleased with the fact that his painting was liked, and with his job as assistant director of San Fernando, and having been made a painter of cartoons, devoted himself with more enthusiasm to painting. He did a good many portraits, for the court and for various corporations around Spain.

In his private life he did not become more ostentatious—except for carriages. The two-wheeler and the gitano horse were given up. He had had enough of them. Instead he got a carriage with four wheels—and good sound mules from Aragon to draw it.

He got a more comfortable house. That was about all.

That May of 1787 he was frantic. "I'm all up in the air," he wrote Zapater. "My wife is sick, the child is worse, and even the cook has fallen ill of a fever." But things got better. He was pleased with the mules and the new carriage.

Zapater says he learned French and that in November he wrote a letter to his uncle in French. One doubts it. For when he went to Bordeaux many years later Moratín said that he could not speak French at all.

In December, 1787, he wrote: "I've become old, with many wrinkles in my face so that you wouldn't know me if it weren't for my flat nose and my sunken eyes. What is certain is that I'm feeling my 41 years mucho, and you probably are as young as you looked at Father Joaquín's school."

He hadn't yet got around to the Carmen for Zapater. He was busy, he said, doing the designs for the tapestry cartoons for the dormitory of the Infantas.

In June it was because he had to paint a picture for Toledo cathedral, the singularly unmoving painting of *Christ Taken Prisoner*. What he wanted, he said, was a little tranquility and a chance to work at the things he enjoyed doing.

IV

Caprichos: The Court of Spain

[1789–1799]

IV
Caprichos: The Court of Spain
[1789-1799]

I

IN THE dawn of the fourteenth of December, 1788, Charles
III died and the younger king who followed him brought into
power a more decadent form of the old régime. Yet it was
this king, Charles IV, who by making Goya court painter in-
advertently established the artist who was to make the most
scathing record of his rule. Within the decade Goya was to
complete the *Caprichos* that are the most famous part of that
record. But not the only part. For every time Goya painted
his sovereigns and the members of their court he made char-
acterizations that the pages of history can only amplify and
use for incomparable illustrations.

In January, 1789—the year the Bastille fell with consequences that were late in reaching Spain, but that did reach
Spain catastrophically, in the end—Charles IV was proclaimed
king. He announced that he would permit the return of bullfighting, which pleased Goya. And in April he made Goya a
court painter—pintor de camara—which pleased him even
more.

Goya could observe the *Caprichos* at the court of Spain
from the inside now. And his own life in that decade between
the year when he was made one of the court painters and the
year at the eighteenth century's end when he was to become

primer pintor de camara, first painter to the king, was filled with *Caprichos* as varied as the ones he drew.

It was the decade when his infatuation with the Duchess of Alba—"El sueño de la mentira y la inconstancia," the dream of lies and inconstancy—reached its height. It was the decade when he painted portraits innumerable of the duchesses, the actresses, the artists, the soldiers, the grandees of Spain. It was the decade when he painted the riotously cheerful murals for San Antonio de la Florida. It was the decade when a ravaging illness left him deafened, outside the world of sound.

One of his own children—a boy of four, named for him—was ill in the spring of 1789, and Goya wrote Zapater that he himself had scarcely lived during that period. But now, thank God, he said, the boy is better, and he could turn his thoughts again to his affairs in the world outside his house, outside the studio where there always seemed to be people wanting to have their portraits painted.

The men arrived in whatever regalia and gold braid they had, the women in laces and jewelry. The men mostly look as though they were bound for masquerades, but the women usually look beautiful. Elie Faure must have had some of Goya's portraits of women in these years in mind when he wrote that Goya "surrounds women with a kind of flaming aureole. They are all beautiful, even the ugly ones." But as Faure himself points out, Goya always showed the true character of the people in the jewels and the regalia, right up to the throne.

Goya's income mounted, though as Mayer has pointed out,

the pay Goya received for his paintings did not increase very much after he became famous. The government paid him 7000 reales for the larger tapestry cartoons, about half that for smaller ones. Between 1783 and 1785 the Bank of Spain bought three large portraits from Goya for 10,000 reales, and paid 4500 for a full-length portrait in life size. The Duke of Osuna paid Goya 12,000 reales for a large family group in 1787. He had paid Goya 4000 reales for two portraits of the king and queen (which Goya learned to turn out wholesale, practically, to fill the vast demand), 6000 reales for half a dozen paintings of Spanish lore, and 10,000 for a group of seven pictures that included the famous *Pradera de San Isidro* outside Madrid.

Jovellanos paid Goya 6000 for the portrait he painted in 1789. But Mayer reminds us that Goya painted portraits of many of his friends for no pay at all. To change from paintings to etchings, we may note that the Duchess of Osuna paid 1500 reales for four sets of the *Caprichos* in 1799. When they were first placed on sale the price was 320 reales a copy, according to the *Diario, de Madrid.*

How can we get an idea of what these sums of money meant? Well, one way is to compare them with the value of labor. In 1786, according to Altamira and Chapman, "the ordinary laborer of Seville earned four and a half reales (about 28 cents) a day; in Barcelona the average was eight reales (50 cents). Agricultural laborers in Andalusia made from three and a half to five reales (22 cents to 33 cents) a day; shepherds got two pounds of bread daily and 160 reales (10 dollars) a year."

In other words, the son of José Goya had come a long way from Fuendetodos. But he still looked at the court of Carlos and Maria Luisa with the eye of a man from Aragon.

2

No court painter ever portrayed his sovereigns more mercilessly than Goya, and few had better reason. Yet it has always been a matter for comment that he was able to show their natures so plainly in his paintings and remain unhung. It may be that when they looked at themselves as Goya saw them and compared his pictures with their inner selves they were relieved to find that he had not overdrawn. How else can one explain the astonishing fact that they actually said they liked some of his portraits of them?

Charles IV was a fool. Maria Luisa was more intricately unadmirable. If it were true that even her lovers hated her we should have added quite a number of men to the great majority who did not like that Queen of Spain. She was dissolute without distinction, and imperious without any saving grace of pride in her country. All in all, she left a name in history that is as unattractive as her face in Goya's paintings of her. The glittering little eyes, the beaky nose and the look of being about to cackle appear, as well, in the *Caprichos*—so clearly, in fact, that one is no more disposed to accept Goya's bland remark that he intended no portrait of any living person in the *Caprichos* than one is disposed to accept the similar observation when it appears on the flyleaf of a novel.

It is all very well for the pure in heart to condemn her; one would expect that. What stands out is that she was condemned by very nearly every one. If we cease asking who

Madrid

DUQUE DE FERNAN NUÑEZ

liked Maria Luisa and ask instead who had any reason to like her, we begin to understand the character behind the face in Goya's paintings.

Goya first knew her when she was Princess of the Asturias, and she had made considerable strides toward deserving her reputation by then. She spent the rest of her years in Spain in living up to it. By the time Napoleon saw her at Bayonne, she was well prepared to give him reason for his remark: "Maria Luisa has her past and her character written on her face, it surpasses anything you dare imagine."[1]

Even as a girl—and girlhood is not easily associated with the raddled face of Maria Luisa's maturity—her nature was not noted for either tranquility or candor. She was a Princess of Parma, a court very close to the throne of Spain. Charles III had ruled there until he was called to assume the Bourbon succession in Madrid. Maria Luisa was betrothed to the son of Charles III when she was a child; the family councils had decided it, and that was that.

The regality of her future did not awe Maria Luisa's brother. Once, in the course of play, he slapped her soundly. With some fury Maria Luisa reminded him of her position. "Well," he said, "then I shall one day be able to boast that I have slapped the Queen of Spain."

It was no great pleasure to her to marry the future Charles IV, and the marriage was a durance she found no more entertaining because she had to spend it under the stern and unfoolable eye of her father-in-law, Charles III. The illusions of Charles III about Maria Luisa were as scant as Charles IV's were boundless.

[1]Sencourt: *The Spanish Crown*. Charles Scribner's Sons.

Once—so runs the tale—the Prince of the Asturias was talking to his father about morality. "It's hard for women of royal rank to commit adultery," he said; "there are so few people of equal rank that they have but little opportunity." To which Charles III replied: "What an ass you are, Carlos, what a blind ass."

And the blindness of Maria Luisa's husband was as much talked about as his wife's copious infidelities. Naturally, since they went together. Whatever scruples about rank Maria Luisa may have had were easily mended in the case of Godoy, the most durable of her lovers. Before his tenure was over he had been raised from a guardsman to the rank of prince, married to a daughter of a Bourbon—so that he could refer to Louis XVI as his step-uncle—and given worldwide power.

Maria Luisa was wayward without being charming, unconventional without being at ease. Villa-Urrutia recalled that she was known as a person "whose appetites the lovers did not satisfy, and whose ardors the years did not cool." Sencourt has said, it is true, that "she added to charm passion, and to passion fury, and to fury wit, and to wit cunning, and to cunning enterprise." That is not half so courtly a remark the second time one reads it over as it seemed the first.

The first of her lovers, according to Sainz de Robles,[1] was Don Eugenio Eulalio Portocarrerro Palafox, Count of Teba, eldest son of the Countess of Montijo, when Maria Luisa was eighteen. Then Don Augustin Lancaster, elderly and over-ripe. He did not last long. The third was Don Juan Pignatelli, a younger son of the Count of Fuentes—here one remembers Fuendetodos—who was supposed to have left the queen for

[1]*Historia y Estampas de la Villa de Madrid.*

love of the Duchess of Alba. The fourth was a mysterious guitarist and guardsman who may or may not have been Godoy's elder brother. The next was Godoy—and after him Don Luis de Urquijo and Don Manuel Mallo are mentioned. Among others.

Goya's *Caprichos* were the scathing reflection of a court whose queen was Maria Luisa. But not his only reflection of that strange time.

3

THE year 1790 was filled with a diversity of commissions, family affairs and travels. Goya was riding the crest of the new reign while across the Pyrenees France was making its Bourbons obsolete. In May he was prosperous enough to ask Zapater to see that his mother had all the money she needed, but Goya hoped that his brothers would be able to look after themselves. The necessity for maintaining a position in Madrid was new to him, and not without its exasperations.

His portrait of Zapater in that year shows a man with a shrewd eye and a cheerful personality. In August Goya went to Valencia for the sea air and his wife's health. He got some hunting in, and he was made a member of the Valencia Academy.

It was probably then that he painted the portrait of a girl called Joaquina Candado. She is said to have been his mistress. The evidence on that point is no more decisive than it is on whether Goya was actually the lover of many other pretty women he painted. It is a straw in the wind of his reputation that so many of them are supposed to have been the mistresses of Goya.

4

FOR GODOY, Spain itself was the golden land of unlimited opportunity. He did not need to sail to the Indies: he stayed at home and dominated them. There was no necessity for him to fight on the sky-lifted plateau of Mexico or convoy the galleons of the king: the treasure was his to share anyway. While other ambitious men went out to plunder continents Godoy was able to conduct his decisive campaigns on a field no larger than a counterpane.

He was undoubtedly the love of Maria Luisa's life; it is less certain that any one but himself was the lifelong love of Godoy. Yet he was generous with his affections. It has been pointed out that he divided them between the Queen (by whom he had royal infantes), his wife (by whom he hoped to have nobles) and his established mistress, Pepita Tudo (by whom he had bastards).

Byron, in one of the Spanish cantos of "Childe Harold," wrote:

How carols now the lusty muleteer?
Of love, romance, devotion is his lay,
As whilome he was wont the leagues to cheer,
His quick bells wildly jingling on the way?
No! as he speeds he chants 'Viva el Rey!'
And checks his song to execrate Godoy,
The royal wittol Charles, and curse the day
When first Spain's queen beheld the black-eyed boy,
And gore-faced Treason sprung from her adulterate joy.

But that was not till some time later on.

Godoy always treated Goya with great deference. He asked Goya to paint his portrait, and in August, 1800, Goya wrote Zapater that he was making a drawing of Godoy on horseback and found the subject about as difficult as any that could be offered to a painter. When you remember the astounding personality of Godoy and remember also that Goya was always concerned with the problem of getting at the character in his subjects' faces, that is easy to understand.

The painting of Godoy was going to take longer than Goya had expected—this was not one of those portraits that he could dash off in an hour. Therefore, Godoy arranged lodgings for Goya at the palace.

It was at Aranjuez, a pleasant place to be in the heat of a Spanish summer, with its cool walks and water gardens. Before Easter it was apt to be too cool.

And from Aranjuez Goya wrote Zapater further about painting Godoy. He said that Godoy had taken him out riding in his carriage. Furthermore, since it was a little chilly, Godoy urged Goya to keep his overcoat on at dinner. And perhaps the greatest honor Godoy paid Goya was to learn to talk with his hands so that he could discourse with the by now stone-deaf Goya, leaving his own food while he gestured. Goya himself, apparently, went right on eating. The food in the house of Godoy would not be anything to leave untasted. Or the wine.

Godoy was sorry to see Goya go. In fact, as Goya wrote Zapater, he had to leave because he had no more canvas to paint on—and no clean shirt. It is apparent that Goya travelled light. Godoy wanted him to stay and paint the minister Saavedra—Sabedra, Goya phonetically writes it—and to remain in Aranjuez until Easter. But Goya was determined to go back to Madrid, and Godoy could not prevent that.

The Spaniards had a nickname for Godoy that was better known than his most famous title as Prince of the Peace. The nickname was El Choricero—the sausagemaker. That was because he was born in Badajoz, in Extremadura, which is the pig-raising region of Spain.—Though one need never rule out the double entendre in looking for the reason behind a Spanish nickname.

By the time he was twenty-five Godoy, thanks entirely to his success with the queen and the king's amiable acquiescence, was premier and foremost power behind the throne of Spain.

He was born in 1767, and he had the good luck to enter the royal bodyguard when he was seventeen. There his guardsman's manner attracted the attention of the Princess of the Asturias, Maria Luisa. It was a memorable moment for Spain. His father was a nobleman, his mother was also noble—and Portuguese. Badajoz, as Jay Allen once reminded us, is very near the border of Portugal.

Godoy was large, indolent, shrewd and able. In Goya's most famous portrait of him he lolls on a couch-shaped rock ledge that is presumably a part of a battlefield and that has always made me suspect that the painting was actually done while Godoy was resting on a sofa.

It was through his older brother, Luis, who was also a guardsman, that Godoy first knew Maria Luisa. The legend is that Luis was a lover of the insatiable Maria Luisa. And that when Luis was sent away to another post—presumably for the good of the realm—he got his brother Manuel to deliver his letters to Maria Luisa. After that Maria Luisa did not miss the brother of Godoy.

The most astounding part of that astounding design for living is that the king, Carlos IV, always seemed to like Godoy.

If it is true that Godoy played a commanding part in the Spain of his time it is also possible to overestimate the value of it. The Count of Torreno, one of his most acute critics, said of Godoy:

"No sooner did he hold out protection to wise and esteemed men than he humbled them. At the same time he was encouraging a special science, establishing a new professorship, or supporting some measure of improvement, he allowed the Marquis of Caballero, a declared enemy to advancement and learning, to trace out a scheme of general public instruction to be adopted in all the universities, which was incoherent and unworthy of the century, permitting him also to make serious omissions and alterations in the codes of law. Although he banished from the court and exiled from the court all those whom he believed to be opposed to him, or who displeased him, as a general rule he did not carry his persecutions any farther, nor was he by nature cruel; he showed himself hard and cruel only with respect to the illustrious Jovellanos; sordid in his avarice, he sold, as if in public auction, offices, magistratures, dignities, sees, sometimes for himself, sometimes for his mistresses, sometimes to satisfy the caprices of the queen." And Sencourt bears him out.

The queen had other favorites after Godoy's interest in power had risen as his interest in her decreased. A young guardsman called Mallo, as we noted, was one of them.

There are many tales about Mallo and the queen in Spain. One story that Stirling-Maxwell and Lady Holland seem to have discovered separately is about the way Mallo tossed around the money the queen gave him. Maria Luisa, the king and Godoy were standing on a balcony at Aranjuez, when Mallo passed by in a resplendent new carriage. "How on earth can that fellow afford better horses than I can?" the king said. The queen colored. "I'm told," she remarked steadily, "that he has a fortune from the Indies." Godoy smiled. "That is not the explanation I've heard around the court," he said. "What have you heard?" the king asked. "I've heard," said Godoy, "that Mallo is kept by a very wealthy and very ugly old woman, whose name I cannot remember."

5

IN A SHOP on a street called the Calle del Desengaño—the Street of Disenchantment, with an appropriateness beyond commentary—the *Caprichos*, in an edition of seventy-two plates, first appeared for sale in the last year of the eighteenth century. The end of an era could not have had a more unsparing epitaph.

The *Caprichos* were on sale for only a few days. Goya was in considerable peril for publishing them, with their lampoons on the powerful and the eminent, at all. The danger came principally from the Inquisitors. Goya himself said that he had been accused before the Inquisition. And there is reason to believe that the Inquisitors were on the point of confiscating the *Caprichos* and proceeding against Goya when the king, who had been talked into accepting the plates for the royal collection, stopped that.

LAS RINDE EL SUEÑO

He had got them together from many drawings done at various times when he saw the town's harlots here or there in Madrid, heard the newest story about the queen and her rivals, remembered pungent episodes of his Aragonese childhood, thought of the devious ways men and women get ahead at court, or tossed in a fever peopled with the phantoms that swarm through the mind when as he said, "the dream of reason produces monsters."

It is preposterous to find in the fantastic plates of the *Caprichos* the extreme mental disorder that some twittering analysts have pretended to see. We have only to look at the serene portraits Goya painted in the same years—the seventeen nineties—to know what nonsense that is. But it would be injudicious not to realize that Goya had been ill during part of the time, tormented by his increasing deafness, and certainly obsessed with the beautiful and tragic Duchess of Alba.

There have been many keys to the *Caprichos*. Goya himself made one. It does not notably improve on the terse captions he originally gave the plates, phrases such as: "What a golden beak" under the sermonizing parrot who holds the fools before him mesmerized, or "God forgive her—that was her mother" for the *maja* turning the old woman away, or "What if the pupil knows more?" for the donkey pompously teaching the smaller ass, or "Don't scream, little fool" for the girl in desperate terror of two cassocked phantoms, or "Lovely mistress!" for the old witch teaching the young one her tricks, or "As far as his grandfather," for the portrait of a donkey looking over the pages of a book holding pictures of his ancestors—a *Capricho* that satirizes the myth of blood purity.

Nearly all the *Capricho* keys have a tendentious way of identifying personages of Charles IV's court in compromising situations. To say they are libelous would be mild; to call them wholesale assassinations of character would miss the mark.

It is not so much that these keys lack data as that they fail in imagination. They poke a few holes in the web of allusion. This one certainly suggests Godoy's affair with the queen; that one may very well burlesque Carnicero's earnest, tedious willingness to paint fat and fatuous marquises as though they were gallant desperadoes. But no one ever believed that poking holes was the most promising way to unravel a web.

Goya himself said that "painting, like poetry, selects from life what she can best use for her own ends. She unites, she concentrates in one fantastic figure circumstances and characters which nature has distributed among various individuals. Thanks to this wise and ingenious combination the artist merits the title of an inventor and ceases to be a mere subordinate copyist."

But, as Mayer observes in commenting on those words, Goya said most precisely what he intended to convey in the *Caprichos* when he announced that he asked the indulgence of the public "in consideration of the fact that the author has made use of no strange models, nor even studies from nature. The imitation of nature is as difficult as it is admirable if one can really attain to it and carry it through. But he also may deserve praise who has completely withdrawn himself from nature and has succeeded in placing before our eyes forms and movements which have hitherto existed only in our imagination."

The question is, and Mayer does not answer it, whose

imagination? What other man would be capable of creating, in etchings that have not been surpassed ever since Goya's time, the astounding world of the *Caprichos*?

It was Juan de la Encina who said that the *Caprichos* really form a picaresque novel. One is inclined to agree with that, since so many adventures of life in eighteenth-century Spain are recorded in the first half of the collection where mountebanks and masqueraders, Calderonian lovers, brigands, friars and fools and men of destiny appear in successive episodes.

But if the first half is picaresque, what are we to call the scenes in the second half of the *Caprichos*? This is a surrealism that makes sense, a satire based on the folklore and the demonology of Aragonese and Castilian tradition. It was this, of course, that stirred Baudelaire to write in the "Fleurs du Mal":

> *Goya, cauchemar plein des choses inconnues*
> *De foetus qu'on fait cuire au milieu des sabbats*
> *Des vielles au miroir et d'enfants toutes nues*
> *Pour tenter les demons ajustant bien leurs bas.*

These cheery reflections perhaps give us a better idea of Baudelaire than of Goya. Sánchez Cantón says, more sensibly and discerningly: "L'auteur traite les démons, dans *les Caprices*, avec une certaine confiance humoristique; il ne les craiant pas, il les situe entre les sorciers et les sorcières qui occu pant alors également ses pinceaux."

The division that Beruete pointed out in the *Caprichos* is valid: He observed that in the first half Goya largely presents human beings acting more or less like demons; in the second half, demons act like human beings. Plate 43, which marks the division, bears the unforgetable inscription—"The dream of reason produces monsters"—under a portrait of Goya asleep at his desk, while the demons of nightmare swarm over his head. It is not, as you see, a precise half-and-half, particularly when you remember that the first edition contained only seventy-two *Caprichos*. But, in general, it is true that the first half presents the follies and brutalities of life in Madrid, the second, the superstitions and phantasms of Spain's folklore. It is here that Goya lashes out at the medieval belief in witchcraft that lived on in the peninsula.

There, Thomas Craven has said, "within the compass of a small piece of copper, Goya focusses his choleric antipathies, his understanding of evil, his universal scorn; in one small ghost story he exposes the superstitious rubbish of old Spain." And: "He weaves his angry spirit into lines that 'live and give life,' into attitudes that quail and sag and die; into masses that move and spin and shudder. His fantastic figures, as he calls them, fill us with a sense of ignoble joy, aggravate our devilish instincts and delight us with the uncharitable ecstasies of destruction. And all this neither wild nor disarrayed, but pressed into design as compact as a bullet!"

Bullet or dagger? Richard Muther thought the etcher's needle was the dagger with which Goya "attacked all that he wished to attack: tyranny, superstition, intrigue, adultery, honor that is sold and beauty that lets itself be bought, the arrogance of the great and the degrading servility of the little. He made an awful and joyful hecatomb of all the vices and scandals of the age. Whomsoever he pilloried was laid bare in all respects; physically and morally, no single trait of him was forgotten. And he did it so wittily that he compelled even the offended person to laugh. Neither Charles IV himself, nor the Court, nor the Inquisition, which bled most beneath his thrusts, dared to complain."

As a matter of fact, they did complain. But without effect. And I have seen priests in Madrid, walking two by two in the Prado, looking at the original drawings from which many of the *Caprichos* were made, and chuckling over Goya's shrewdest thrusts.

6

SATIRE is no novelty to the Spaniard. As John Dos Passos once said in a note on the finest Spanish artist since Goya, Luis Quintanilla, the greatest works of art in Spain have always been done by satirists. You have only to think of Cervantes to see the point of that observation. Long before the *Caprichos* Madrid had seen many a satiric artist come and go. But never on the plane of Goya. Murther says that in the *Caprichos* "Goya stands revealed as a figure without even a forerunner in the history of art," which is a needless superlative. But he goes on to say: "Satirical representations of popular superstitions, bitter, mordant attacks on the aristocracy, the government, all social conditions, unprecedented attacks on the crown, on religion and its doctrines, inexorable satires upon the Inquisition and all the monastic orders, make up this most remarkable book." Goya remained friendly with the Church, which continued to give him commissions to the end of his days. So we need not believe from Muther's suggestion that he became a howling atheist. Yet he was fearless and unsparing in his satires on what was manifestly corrupt. The point is that there was no answering Goya, ever.

The *Caprichos* present, on one plane, a decadent and corrupt court, a part of the life of late eighteenth-century Madrid, with all the faults of the time, it is true, but also with all the pride. It is a Castilian world, and it has the Castilian manner. These caricatures are savage, but they show a cultivated people—which makes the scorn of their absurdities all the more stinging.

On another plane, the *Caprichos* present another world: the supernatural tradition of Aragon. For there is, it seems to me, a distinction worth noting in the spirit, as well as in the matter, of the *Caprichos*. The realistic scenes are peopled with the characters of Madrid; the supernatural ones are peopled with the characters of the Aragonese demonology. Goya saw reality with the eyes of a man who had by then spent most of his life in Madrid; indeed, he was more *madrileño* than most men born in the coronada villa. But when he drew the barbarous phantoms of the later *Caprichos* he drew with the memory of childhood, the tales of frightening sorceries he had heard long ago in Fuendetodos.

These hair-raising apparitions haunted him all his life. It is not only in the *Caprichos* he drew them. In paintings as well as in sketches and etchings you see again and again the preoccupation with the supernatural that eternally crops out: the hounds of Hell with bodies of men and heads of dogs, the Great Goat holding midnight court with broom-riding hags that bring infants to their unholy rites, the outrageous owls and cat-headed birds of prey and darkness. Surely there is enough here to provide a remarkable field for the study of the mind of Goya. He laughed at these things, it is true. He spoke out against the ignorance that bred these superstitions.

Yet one wonders whether he himself was completely free

from a kind of unwilling belief in them. They were always somewhere in his mind, a part of the inherited substance of his being.

Indeed, students of lycanthropy and other forms of demonism have found some revealing illustrations in the works of Goya. According to Grillot de Givry, "It is apparent that the Spanish master was well informed on points of sorcery, and this is no matter for astonishment, since Spain began to be a country of witches a very long time ago and still is so today. We learn from Guillaume Le Breton that sorcerers who foretold the future were found there as early as the thirteenth century—in the time of the Countess Matilda, who consulted them habitually—and then, at the beginning of the nineteenth century, we quite unexpectedly come across this picture by Goya in direct line with the dimmest ages of sorcery."[1] In the same way, one might say that to encounter a man tipping his hat is to come across something in the direct line of chivalry.

The picture that struck Grillot de Givry is Goya's painting of the sorcerers' kitchen that once belonged to the Osunas. It has a miniature fearsomeness about it that suggests the decorative legend rather than the lash of satire. Five gentleman demons—or is the one with the back turned a lady?—are off on a spree. They are in various stages of transformation. One stoops over the bowl of magic brew. One is already half animal. Two are waiting their turns. And one, turned into a black goat riding a broomstick, is already soaring up the chimney toward the night's assignation.

[1]*Witchcraft, Magic and Alchemy.* By Grillot de Givry. Houghton Mifflin Company. 1931.

Two skulls lie on the floor, and various bones hang on a line beside a flaring light. The transformation of the witches or sorcerers into animal form, Guillot de Givry explains, "took place at the moment of passing under the chimney mantel, sometimes even a little sooner." And sometimes, apparently, no chimney was needed at all. In the *Capricho* called "Aguarda que te unten"—"Wait till you've been anointed," for example, the event takes place in some chimneyless space. Here the demon has become all goat, except for the one human foot that the impassive fellow-demon with the anointing bowl is holding.

In this *Capricho*—as in others where the rites of sorcery appear—Goya used his knowledge of Spain's witch-haunted lore to satirize the rites and customs of his own day. And this, I believe, is one of the main reasons why the powers of the Inquisition were turned against the *Caprichos*. For the Inquisitors, dedicated to stamping out witchcraft, might be furiously aware that Goya was satirizing things they defended while apparently joining them in attacking the older sorcery.

Goya could not have used the superstitions of the past to attack the follies of the present with such incomparable effect if he were not thoroughly familiar with the beliefs in broom-riding midwives surrounded by the images of infants, night-prowling visitants and phantoms winged and horned. And it was not at all a matter of antiquity. Witchcraft, for that matter, was still believed in throughout Spain in Goya's day, and the Inquisitors persecuted the belief savagely. Within the decade that Goya made the *Caprichos* the Inquisition burned a woman accused of witchcraft in Seville.

The life of the town satirized in the *Caprichos* is rather like the life of the town satirized in the *sainetes*—short, salty, raffish plays—of Ramon de la Cruz. Cruz began as the first man to translate Shakespeare into Spanish, Fitzmaurice-Kelly has observed, and finding that his talents as a tragic writer did not set even the small Manzanares River on fire turned to writing the *sainetes*—originally comic interludes that presently became one-act comedies of popular manners—that he could contrive in inexhaustible quantities on such themes as gay prelates, shrewd country cousins outwitting the worldly vultures at court, the *chisperos*, *majos* and *majas* of the Lavapies quarter: in short, the people of Madrid.

The pungent wit and the caustic observation of Cruz's *sainetes* give them a good deal in common with the *Caprichos* of Goya. One need not go to them in the cerements of research to appreciate Fitzmaurice-Kelly's remark that they form "a huge whispering gallery where you can hear all the political and social gossip of the day: all the middle and lower classes of Madrid flit past you, in a vivid and picturesque panorama, lighthearted, careless, full of impertinent grace and wit." In defense of Cruz and his *sainetes* one may plead, beyond the fact that they lack the deeper force of the *Caprichos* and have not Goya's fury, that they could not in any case hope to have the same universal idiom that one of the *Caprichos* has when it is hung on any wall in any country in any age.

7

ON THE high scaffolding, getting paint in his eyes and probably using language as uncustomary to the church as his manner of painting was to the faith, Goya decorated San Antonio

de la Florida with murals of a very eighteenth-century St.
Anthony of Padua performing a miracle before a very
worldly crowd of Madrileños.

Ventura Rodriguez, the distinguished architect and a
friend of Goya, had rebuilt the little church for the king. It
is just large enough to have held the court circle of Charles
IV's time when the king was at the Casa del Campo. At the
edge of the great park where the king hunted day after day,
a very short drive by carriage from the royal palace, San
Antonio stands across the road from the Manzanares on the
Moncloa road. Goya worked at the murals—they are not true
frescoes, rather tempera—in the late summer of 1798. A bill
for sponges that Beruete discovered, suggests, if it does not
absolutely prove, how Goya got done so large a work in such
a remarkably short time. They were begun in July and finished by the end of October. The sponges were tied to the end
of long sticks, dipped in color, and used to paint wide surfaces.
Whether his mind was filled with memories of Tiepolo, Cor-
reggio and Mantegna's murals, as some have suggested, Goya
made the scene supremely his own as he worked swiftly
through the hot weather and into the months when the sharp
Madrid autumn was beginning. In the winter the air under
the dome that has been smoked by fires in the war would have
been stingingly cold. The Duchess of Alba may have stopped
her carriage on the way from Madrid to her miniature palace
at Moncloa in the hills beyond the present University City to
watch Goya at work, paint-spattered on the scaffolding. The
tradition has always been that he painted her into one of the
groups around the saint.

The girl in the red skirt: that, one is told, is *la Maja de*

Goya. There is some resemblance to the beautiful, wayward Duchess who was loved by the people and looked at askance by the nobility. And the woman under San Isidro's outstretched hand, that, they say, is the wife of Goya.

There are many tales about those murals at San Antonio. One is that when the king came and looked up at the dome he recognized many faces, and that he turned to Goya and said:

"I told you to make the murals gay and aristocratic, and you've painted in all the trollops in Madrid."

"Precisely," said Goya.

The theme of the murals is St. Anthony of Padua raising a dead man from the grave, so that he can confront his murderer. Goya translated the story into the idiom of eighteenth-century Madrid. If the members of the board of works of Pilar Cathedral, who had long ago objected to some of Goya's designs on the ground that they were too worldly, saw the murals in San Antonio de la Florida, they must have smiled grimly, their worst suspicions confirmed. With Asensio Julia as his assistant he painted the saint performing the miracle. But the crowd clustered along the painted railing that holds the whole composition together is interested in more mundane affairs.

That lively crowd is far more interested in looking down at the people in the church below than in looking at the saint and his miracle. They are Madrileños of Goya's day, of all degrees of society and of all ages. There are many children, some of them with their legs perilously over the railing that holds the crowd on high. Blue, rose, brown, gold, red and gray, the colors are very bright, the women spirited and pretty, the men arrogant and watchful. They are all, as Stokes remarked, "clearly out for a romp." He compared them to figurantes in a ballet, and added that "the frescoes of San Antonio de la Florida are in art what Offenbach is in music." I should rather say, Mozart.

St. Anthony in his friar's habit stands on a chair and duly brings back the man from death. Goya may have used sponges in painting the walls. But not on the faces of those girls in gold and rose, the colors that are in the paintings of the *Maja Dressed* and the *Maja Naked*. There are men in blue coats among them, yet they belong to the background, it is the girls you look at, the girls in mantillas behind the skyed railing, laughing down at worshippers who change with the generations, while they are changeless.

And around the dome on the arches and in the niches there are trumpeting angels, dressed in gold and scarlet, brunettes as well as blondes but somehow more blondes, flushed and confident and happy. After looking at them all, Gomez de la Serna remarked: "St. Anthony is reviving a man in the process of decomposition in these murals; Goya revives an epoch that is completely gone."

V

The Dream of Lies and Inconstancy

V

The Dream of Lies and Inconstancy

I

HER FACE haunts Goya's art. Not only in his famous paintings of her in the white dress and the scarlet sash or in the mantilla with the Andalusian landscape beyond, but in etchings and drawings innumerable that show her dark hair and lovely arrogant face. She is apart from all other women in the chronicle of Goya. When the days of revelry were over he damned her to hell in the etching of the woman with two faces, called the *Dream of Lies and Inconstancy*. But he could never burn her out of his mind. For the rest of his life, wherever he drew, again and again her face appears.

She became Duchess of Alba at fourteen when her grandfather died in the year of America's independence. Thirteenth Duchess of Alba, last of the line in direct succession, and married to something negligible and imperially rich. It is a theme for all romanticists, and they have made the most of it.

When Lady Holland wrote about her in the journal of her Spanish travels at the beginning of the nineteenth century she was already a legend. "The matadores are the toreros admired by the ladies. The Duchesses of Osuna and Alba formerly were rivals for Pedro Romero." She added that however the Duchess of Alba may have indulged herself, she "never wantonly violated decency in conversation or deportment." There are tales of the queen's malicious envy, and how the Duchess repaid it by dressing her maids in replicas of the new gowns the queen had ordered from Paris and sending them to promenade in carriages on the Prado, to amuse all Madrid with the parody. And of fire breaking out twice in her palace on gala occasions, so that she suspected her enemies and at the climax of the next gala said: "I do not care to leave to others the pleasure of burning this house. This time, I think I shall start the flames myself."

These are the fantasies of admiring wits; truer as atmosphere than as truth, told always to those who stand before Goya's portraits of her. She did not write or paint or create; she was one of those women who inspire these arts enormously in others, not Goya alone.

2

Goya's magnificent paintings of the *Maja Dressed* and the *Maja Naked* are forever associated with her name. The *Maja Dressed* wears a thin white torero costume, her arms behind her head on the green divan, and at her shoulders the butterfly pattern he drew years before in the *Capricho* of a woman very like her borne upward by three bullfighters. The *Maja Naked* is in all but costume a replica, though the light is closer to the shine of day, as though it had been painted in the open air.

The legend of the *Maja Naked* and the *Maja Dressed* is a favorite part of the apocrypha of Goya. It will always be as futile to try to dispel the belief that they represent the Duchess of Alba as it will be to try to dispel the flagrant rumors of Goya's adventures in Rome, the tales of a guitar-and-dagger-haunted young manhood, or the story that he once took a fowling piece to the Duke of Wellington.

THE MAJA NAKED

THE MAJA DRESSED

Madrileños believe that they were not painted at the same time, that the *Maja Naked* was painted first, and that whispers about it went around. The tale reached the Duke, her husband, and he was in a murderous rage about it. He rushed to horse and set out for vengeance, planning to saber Goya for his audacity. Goya heard he was coming, from afar. He put the painting away, and in no time at all painted the picture of *Maja Dressed*. The Duke came roaring into Goya's studio. "I hear, sir, that you have painted a portrait of my wife naked." "Not at all," Goya said coolly—all versions of the invention agree that Goya was very cool about it—"there is my portrait of your wife." He pointed to the only visible one —the *Maja Dressed*. "And it has not your wife's features, anyway." Which is true. But the story is not. There is no shred of evidence on earth for it. And even if there were, who could believe, looking at Goya's portrait of the Duke bending listlessly over a piano with a quartet by Haydn in his hands, that he could be capable of such fiery talk.

The two paintings once belonged to Godoy. They were taken from him with all his enormous wealth after the fiasco at Aranjuez, and listed as *Gitanas*. The last Prado commentary on them discussed them with a kind of severe lyricism: *La Maja Desnuda—De cuerpo entero, acostada en una otomana tapizada de azul* (though it always seemed darker in the Prado's light); *sábana blanca, como las almohadas. La Maja Vestida—De cuerpo entero; viste de blanco y chaquetilla amarilla con adornos negros; cinturón ancho color de rosa. La otomana tapizado de verde; colcha blanca.* And denial that they represent the Duchess of Alba as well as the suggestion that they could be of two different women appears in the firm remark: "Es indudable que la Duquesa de Alba no sirvió de modelo para ninguna de ellas."

They were painted, certainly, late in the eighteenth century; perhaps in 1797 or 1798. I am inclined to agree with Mayer that there can be no doubt that they both represent the same person; they are obviously companion pieces. And the fact that they belonged to Godoy only recalls the fact that Godoy helped himself to the possessions of the Duchess of Alba at the time of her death. And so again we come to the shadowy possibility that the legend may be true.

They were painted in the years at the century's turn when Goya was in the full flight of his own romanticism, painting the impious carnival for the dome of San Francisco de la Florida, and many scenes of the diversions of the *majos* and *majas* of Madrid. These characters of balcony scenes and tableau portraits are in a kind of masquerade, for, as Beruete explained, "the *majos* and *majas* are those persons who at the end of the eighteenth century and the beginning of the nineteenth adopted the popular costume, at that time very similar to that used by the *toreros*. Very shortly afterwards this picturesque dress became generally used by all classes of society, including—one might even say preferentially by—the aristocratic class." Madrazo always insisted that the *Majas* were posed by a girl who enjoyed the "protection" of Padre Bravi, a friend of Goya, and that Goya's grandson told him they were not of the Duchess.

3

THE sketches he made of her in his notebook of the journey to Sanlúcar are far more important as records of their intimacy. And Goya wrote to Zapater:

[126]

"It would be better for you to come and help me paint la de Alba, who came into my studio to have her face painted, and came out with that; certainly it gives me more pleasure than painting on canvas, and I am also to paint her at full length, and she'll come for that as soon as I finish a drawing I'm doing of the Duque de la Alcudia on horseback."

The Duque de la Alcudia was Godoy, who had, as you will remember, been chosen by the queen as prime minister, on grounds, as Madariaga remarked, "best known to herself and everybody else but her husband." The queen wrote venomously to Godoy about her—"By tonight the de Alba will have gone, as crazy as in her springtime of youth"—and, a little later, she said the Duchess and all her works should be buried in oblivion.[1]

Goya's deafness is romantically associated with the journey to the Duchess' palace in Sanlúcar, in Andalusia. Here again certitude's pavement ends. The Duchess, the tale that turns up over and over again tells, had been banished from court for her escapades. Goya went with her. They travelled over the brigand-strewn roads of Spain in a carriage. In the night time, at Despeña Perros, the coach collapsed, the axle hopelessly bent by a rock in the way. Goya jumped out. The coachman said he could do nothing. Goya said: "I can." It was a cold night, and Goya caught a chill that led to his deafness in it, though they were all glad of the great fire he made. Over that fire he heated the axle to the color of coral. Then, with his own hands, he bent it back into shape. The axle was cooled, and put back in the carriage. Goya and the Duchess rolled on to Sanlúcar.

[1]*Cartas Confidenciales de La Reina Maria Luisa y de Don Manuel Godoy.* Carlos Pereyra. Madrid.

The tale has the charm of completeness and the undeniable trait of immortality. It may be told for these sound reasons—but never as truth. For Goya's deafness had roots that must be traced deviously through his personal history, and exemplified in some of the searing paintings he put on the walls of his house, the *Quinta del Sordo*, later on. It is not through such fantastic episodes that one may arrive at the causes—and the crucial consequences—of Goya's years of desperation.

It may be that the Duchess went to Sanlúcar to observe a period of mourning for her husband. He died in Seville on June 9, 1796. Seville is not far from Sanlúcar.

Goya, at any rate, was apparently away from Madrid from the beginning of October, 1796, to the early part of the following year. Sánchez Cantón believes that Goya did not return to Madrid until April, 1797.

The evidence of Goya's return to Madrid, at that time, is that it was then—in April, 1797—that he resigned as Director of Painting at the Academy of San Fernando. The Academy accepted his resignation, which was offered on grounds of ill health—particularly Goya's increasing deafness. A note in the Calleja collection of Goya's works says that Goya was named honorary general director of the Academy at the end of April. Yet it was in 1797 that Goya painted a portrait of his old friend, Zapater, and a portrait of the liberal man of letters, Melendez Valdez, "Poeta Español," that links him once more to the freer intellectual elements of his time.

4

GOYA first knew the Duchess of Alba in the years when he was painting the bright pageantry of the cartoons for tap-

THE DUCHESS OF ALBA

estries. Her silhouette has been identified in the scene of the
maja and the cloaked and sworded gallants of the Paseo en
Andalusia. There she is a girl, enchanted and a little frightened to be with four such grim and desperate-looking men.
He knew her by reputation: famous in Madrid, and a patroness of the bullfighters.

He saw her at the Alameda, the country place of the
Duchess of Osuna, and again one sees her face and figure in
the painting of the swing, and in the tableau of the riders
gathered around a girl who has fallen from her mule, while
one beauty raises her hands to the high heavens with delighted
grief. Everything is all very artificial and fête galante. One
would never believe from such light and irresponsible paintings as these that the same Goya was to paint the incomparable battle scene of the Dos de Mayo when Murat's mamelukes charged the people of Madrid, or the searing *Desastres*
etchings of the backwash of war. But those years were still far
ahead, and she did not see them. She died still young—
poisoned, some said—in the summer of 1802.

Her spirit and her willfulness are in Goya's portraits of
her, and they can only be italicized by our knowledge that she
loved action more than reflection, gayety more than contem-
plation, and the company of Goya or the *diestro* Costillares
more than her husband. She was extravagant, she was
haughty, she was beautiful. Her extravagance was tempered
by generosity, her haughtiness by wit, and her beauty needed
no tempering at all. She scorned the frayed brocades of Spain's
court-bound aristocracy, and because she was the Duchess of
Alba she could do that with impunity, since she outranked
them all. Beruete's judgment is a little on the side of the

dueñas when he speaks of her relations with Goya. But when he says her independence and her unconventionality won her "the sympathy of the people, the amazement of the middle class, and the hatred of her equals, the nobility," he is true to her life. So many men within that lifetime tried to be, and she tried so many.

She stirred Goya to art as no other woman ever did, even in desperation. If his most light-hearted testament of their intimacy is in the Sanlúcar sketch book, the best is in the mantilla portrait, where she stands, pointing to the inscription he has written for her in the sand beneath her Arab-pointed slippers, and wearing two rings: his name on one, hers on the other.

These, and the letter to Zapater, and the stories of the journey to Sanlúcar, with all the undocumented tales of their love affair may point conclusively, but the proof that they were lovers was not drawn up and signed before a notary in their lifetime. It is a question that has inordinately interested those scholars who scorn with upturned noses the tales of men's love of women in today's public prints—and bury them in those of the past.[1] The difference in their ages can be given any weight you like.

Goya's drawing of the Duchess with the dark child—La Negrita Maria de la Luz—who was her ward at Sanlúcar is

---

[1]*Interlude.* A Scene in Elysium. Goya and the Duchess stand talking together. She does not read any of the books that through a century and a half have discussed them; she was never much on reading, anyway. But Goya tells her about them:

THE DUCHESS: Have they found anything new?
GOYA: A little; some of it I'd forgotten myself.
THE DUCHESS: But the same question still bothers them?
GOYA: It still drives them frantic.
THE DUCHESS: What a waste of time.
GOYA: But how they enjoy it!

not the only one he made. There are others, the one of the siesta, with her face turned, so that one cannot finally say these are her features. There is the painting of the Duchess frightening her nana, a crucifix aloft to ward off devils and all evil things, and the painting of the two children—it was the boy, Niño Luis de Berganza, she wrote to,[1] not Maria de la Luz—trailing the same nana like pages at a coronation. The Madrazo Album contains more sketches that recall again the wide eyes and the oval face, and the sketch of the Duchess dressing her hair might be an illustration for the fatuous rodomontade a French marquis, Fleurot de Langle, wrote about her in his account of travels in Spain:

"The Duchess of Alba has not a hair in her head that does not stir desire. Nothing on earth is as lovely as she is; impossible to surpass her. When she goes down the street all the world is at the windows to gaze, and little children stop playing games to see her."

If they were playing at bullfighting as Spanish children have for generations, wearing the wickerwork bull in turn, as they do in one of Goya's tapestry cartoons, the Duchess might join their sport. She knew it well. Her bulls were in the ring at Seville. She was a partisan of Costillares, we are told, and his celebrity has not yet faded; he invented the volapie and the veronica. The rest of the court mainly favored his rival, Pepe-Hillo. She also liked José Romero, as Lady Holland said, and Goya painted him wearing a costume the Duchess gave him. In that painting Romero, brother of the famous Pedro, wears a cape in the colors of Jerez, around his neck a handkerchief from Ronda, and on his

[1] *La Duquesa de Alba y Goya.* By Joaquín Ezquerra del Bayo. Madrid. 1928.

head a Sevillano band, all in honor of his triumphs in those towns.

Her titles were as many as her names—these begin with Maria del Pilar Teresa Cayetana de Silva Alvarez de Toledo, and go on for some lines after that—and she had houses and palaces for many of them, strewn around Spain. In Madrid they were palaces, and just outside the town, in the trees of the hill at Moncloa, there was a miniature palace, a *palacete*, a fabulous place, a kind of rococo doll's house, bright with priceless decorations in the Neapolitan manner. In the alcove of her bedroom Roman goddesses stand as pilasters on either side of her bed, and they bear candle holders, though it seems an odd idea to have fastened them squarely on the goddesses' pretty breasts. The walls of the alcove are painted to show windows looking on a painted garden by day; in the dressing room beyond the frescoes show a garden by night.

The imperious red granite head of Goya by Juan Cristobal stands on a column beside San Antonio de la Florida. His face is turned toward the Moncloa road, and Madrileños say he is waiting for the Duchess, who is late, to drive down in her carriage.

5

GOYA's deafness made an enormous and decisive difference in his life. And an intense difference in his art. There is a truth beyond documentation in Mayer's remark that "If deafness had not forced Goya to talk by sign language for almost half his long life, he might never have learned to draw the most keenly observed and expressive hands since Rembrandt." Yet a posterity that forever finds new meanings in Goya's art will

also probably forever find new significances in the state of
health behind it.

He has been called mad—but never by any of the Spaniards
who knew Goya and who left written records of him. He
has offered a distinguished target for the varieties of medical
speculation. His deafness has been explained—clinically—as
due to avariosis, which is a timid suggestion that one of the
pretty Spanish girls he slept with may have given him a start
toward deafness. It has been explained—romantically—as due
to a chill caught on the night of the immortal journey with
the Duchess of Alba to Sanlúcar.

Whatever Goya did he did with a certain violence. When
he got sick he got sick in character. He was not merely ill.
He was fabulously distraught. Of his periods of sickness he
wrote with vigor when he addressed Zapater: "I'm so frantic
I can scarcely stand myself"—and he painted with no less
vigor when he made that picture of himself attended by
Doctor Arrieta. There he made himself the sickest-looking
man in all art. The anguish he could never get into his
Crucifixion is in his own face while the doctor bends over
him offering an oversize tumbler of something doubtless very
antiseptic.

Goya made his illnesses spectacular. And their effect was
drastic. But for a man who lived to be eighty-two he wasn't
really ill very often. And, obviously, any man who could live
to be eighty-two such violent years as Goya did must have
had a remarkably powerful constitution. That was a tribute to
his peasant stock, his Aragonese stubbornness, if you will,
and his character. Demons were never very far from Goya's
mind. They swarm, bat-winged, eerily grinning and diaboli-

cal, all through his art. He did not take them passively. He fought them. But they were there.

Particularly the demons of ill-health. It was always a challenge to him to work harder. Earlier it has been pointed out that Goya's series of etchings were done when he was sick. They always go together, the Velasquez series and one illness: the *Caprichos*, the *Disparates*, the *Desastres*, the *Tauromaquia* and other periods of bad health.

Up to the time he was thirty, Goya apparently wasn't ill much. Then, in 1777, when he was thirty-one, he told Zapater that he was recovering from "a grave illness." He hoped he had escaped for good. But in 1784, at thirty-eight, he reported that he was feeling very low, "I have lost all strength and work very little." And the worst was yet to come. In 1792, when he was forty-six, he was severely ill again, and the following year he had a touch of apoplexy that laid him low. For the next year—1794—he was sick enough so that he had to give up work, and in 1797, when he was fifty-one, he had to resign from the Academy because he couldn't go on with his work there. This was the most severe of his illnesses until 1819, when he was seventy-three, the year he painted himself with Arrieta.

Goya never said what made him deaf. That opens the way to two probabilities. That he did not know, which is the simple and decisive one. That he knew and did not want to say, which lets every one else suggest just what caused it. And in such a field for suggestion there are wide latitudes.

The romantic story of the Duchess of Alba's journey is suspect as all romanticizing is suspect. We don't know that it ever took place at all. As to whether Goya could have become deaf as a result of a chill caught when he gallantly got out and made the fire to straighten the bent axle, one can only point out that it might well have been a cause. It is the event, not the diagnosis, that is derelict.

Goya referred to his deafness from time to time. When he went to paint Godoy, in 1800, Godoy asked him to stay to dinner. And, we recall, Godoy learned to use sign language so that he could make himself understood to the painter.

Zapater went to Fuendetodos when he was writing about Goya. He found in the village old people who remembered Goya when he went back there between the two sieges of Zaragoza. They recalled, these ancients, as Zapater called them, that Goya spoke to his servant through a sign language that is still in existence.

And as an old man, in the soundless exile on the quays of Bordeaux, Goya was furious at Brugada: "Can't you make your gestures more discreetly? Do you take pleasure in allowing every one to see that old Goya is neither able to walk nor hear?"

The physicians have made Goya's deafness into a theme for the artistic monographs of their leisure. Sánchez Cantón observes that Villanueva's monograph is full of inaccuracies. But Sánchez de Rivera[1] has made such a full and entirely ingenious case, based on circumstantial evidence, for his avariosis theory, that it deserves some attention. Mayer's vague idea that Goya fell ill of something contributory in Fuendetodos has not enough substance for discussion.

The avariosis theory is based on a judicious series of tendentious quotations from his letters to Zapater—and a letter

[1] *La Enfermedad de Goya.* Daniel Sánchez de Rivera. Madrid. 1935.

or two by others—and a determined interpretation of the supernal elements in his art. That his deafness was a tortuous and darkening and deepening adventure no one who has experienced or who has thought about deafness can want to deny. Yet I am not aware of Mayer's basis for the remark that Goya's severe illness not only "damaged his sense of hearing" but also "weakened his eyesight."

Only Aguilera,[1] in a brilliant, three-peseta pamphlet on the Pinturas Negras, has commented upon Sánchez de Rivera. He treats it with a certain seriousness, but he is quick to point out that Goya, with all the disasters he had to sustain to win through to triumph, had plenty of cause for his black moods. No one knows with ultimate certainty what caused the deafness of Goya.

6

THE Duchess of Alba is supreme in Goya's gallery of women, but decidedly she is not alone. For as Mayer has said in an eloquent passage, Goya, whose genius was as comprehensive as it was powerful, was creative above all other artists in painting the women of Spain.

"With what depth of human feeling [Mayer wrote], what a wealth of various figures in drawings, etchings and lithographs, in pictures large and small, in single portraits and in groups, in wall paintings and in tapestry cartoons, Goya has painted the girl just grown, the toothless old woman, young women like blossoms and tender dreams, resigned old age, the sentimentality and visionary melancholy of youth, the pride of beautiful women in their prime, the tyrannical

[1]*Las Pinturas Negras de Goya.* Emiliano M. Aguilera. Madrid. 1936.

THE DUCHESS OF ALBA

VOLAVE

disposition of ageing ladies, the desperate fight of beauties on the wane to preserve their looks and the old hag's half tragic, half comic love of finery! He painted queens and milkmaids, the flower of the Spanish aristocracy, great duchesses and women of lowly birth, the wives of burghers and chamber-maids, respectable matrons and actresses, singers and majas. He painted innocence and vice, seduction and devotion, lust of power and martyrdom, the mother and the harlot, simplicity and love of finery, vanity and modesty, the blue stocking and the little goose, the angel and the shrew, heedless levity and solid worth, the heroine and the destroyer, the working woman and the woman living for enjoyment, the brutal woman and the tender, the fiery and the gentle. And he painted that ideal of womanhood as described in Cervantes, the Spanish woman, who is 'an angel in church, a lady in the street and a devil incarnate in bed.' "[1]

Goya always had an eye for pretty women. He liked them, and they liked him, and he enjoyed painting them. In contrast to the fantastic beldams of the *Caprichos* and other grotesques, the loveliness of some of the women in his gallery of portraits and in many of the sketches is unforgetable. Yet a young Englishman called Henry Swinburne, ancestor of the laureate of *Dolores*, who travelled in Spain in 1775 and 1776[2] found Spanish women "in general little and thin; few are strikingly beautiful, but almost all have striking black eyes, full of expression." Mr. Swinburne observed that Spanish women "are endowed by nature with a great deal of wit and

[1]*Francisco de Goya.* By A. L. Mayer. Translated by Robert West. London & Toronto: J. M. Dent & Sons, Ltd. 1924.
[2]*Travels Through Spain.* By Henry Swinburne, Esq. London: Printed by J. Davis, for P. Elmsly in the Strand. 1787.

lively repartee, but for want of the succours of education, their wit remains obscured by the rudest ignorance, and the most ridiculous prejudices."

Growing a little sharper, with an edge of asperity to his remarks that makes one wonder what in the world the Spanish beauties could have done to Mr. Swinburne to make him sound so nettled, he says of them that "their tempers never having been fashioned by polite intercourse nor softened by the necessary contradiction, are extremely pettish and violent." Poor Mr. Swinburne. It is surprising that he enjoyed himself at all in Goya's Spain, where, all other testimony to the contrary, the women "are continually pouting for something or other, and put out of humour by the merest trifles. Most of the ladies about court are the reverse of handsome," he thought.

Goya did not. He painted beauties wherever he could find them. He found more in streets far from the palace, on the paseos and in village squares, than at court. Maria Luisa did not like beautiful women around her; they emphasized the obvious.

But they were not all ugly duchesses. Goya found some lovely faces among the aristocracy of Madrid. Many of them are in the tapestry cartoons—for though these are scenes of popular life the carefree characters are masqueraders, and their bright costumes have all the realism of a fancy-dress ball. Ezquerra del Bayo has seen among them the faces of the Duchess of Alba and the Duchess of Osuna. This might be expected; what is more to the point is that Goya, as we have seen, made them look as duchesses would look if they were dressed as peasant girls.

The portraits of the Duchess of Alba that Goya painted

are their own testament of beauty. He painted the Marquesa de Santa Cruz reclining on a couch almost in the attitude of the *Maja Naked* and the *Maja Dressed*, Moorish-pointed slippers on her feet and leaves of wild grape in her hair. There is his portrait of the Countess of Haro, dark-eyed and insolently young, and his portrait of the Duchess of Abrantes when she was full-blown. There is the portrait of the Marquesa de Santiago, standing on a romantic heath, looking bold as her reputation, and as wayward.

The Marquesa de Pontejos stands astonishingly caparisoned in silks and ribbons and laces to make one of Goya's most brilliant portraits. She holds a decorative flower preposterously— as though it were made of metal and the metal lightly charged with electricity. Every benefit of costume, background, posture, Goya gave her; she has all the attributes of beauty and few of the looks. Caricature lies behind the characterization. There is a suggestion in the portrait that she wanted to be painted as Goya had painted the Duchess of Alba. And, as in the Liria portrait of the Duchess of Alba, the Marquesa de Pontejos stands, full-length against a pleasant country background, one arm half extended, one arm at her side. Even the dog is there, in both pictures. But the Duchess of Alba has a decorative Pomeranian. The Marquesa de Pontejos has a pug.

It is the contrast between what Mr. Swinburne saw on his tour of Spain and what Goya shows us that dramatizes Goya's view of life. Nothing could be more illuminating than the confrontation. Yet at times Mr. Swinburne exposes the follies of the court in a way that shows what a rich field for social satire Goya had when he produced the *Caprichos*.

Still smarting, Swinburne says that the women "do not seem to have any ambition of passing for clever or accomplished; not one talent do they possess; nor do they ever work, read, write, or touch any musical instrument: their *cortejo*, or gallant, seems to be their only plaything." It is odd that he should not mention the patronage of art.

At the court, in Charles III's time, no one would suggest that all sides of Spain were represented. It was after seeing the lives of the courtiers that Swinburne wrote: "I believe no country exhibits more bare-faced amours, and such an appearance of indelicate debauchery as this. The account given me of their manner of living in their family way, as soon as they come out of the convent, and before they have fixed upon a lover to fill up their time more agreeably, is as follows: they rise late, and loiter away the remains of the morning among their attendants, or wear it out at church in a long bead-roll of habitual unmeaning prayers; they dine sparingly, sleep, and then dress or saunter for a couple of hours on the Prado. They are never without some sort of sugar-plum or high-spiced comfit in their mouths. As soon as it is dark, they run to the house of some elderly female relation, where they all huddle together over a pan of coals, and would not for the world approach the company that may occasionally drop in; it would throw them into the greatest confusion were they to be requested to join in the conversation. The hour of assembly passed, they hurry home to their maids, and with their help, set about dressing their own suppers by way of amusement." In arriving at that dour view of the lives of the jeunes filles en fleur Mr. Swinburne has no time for looking into the rules of church and court that governed them.

7

THERE are many other tales of oher ladies in the *leyenda Goyesca*. The ladies are usually anonymous. One is indebted to Matheron and others for the story of the beautiful noble-woman of Madrid who wanted very much to have Goya paint her portrait. Improbably enough, Goya was not at first interested. Her husband, no doubt a marquis, went to Goya and asked him to paint the portrait. But Goya, who would never paint any one he did not want to paint, still said no. Even that did not daunt the two. And, finally, the husband thought up a way.

He brought his beautiful wife to Goya's studio when no one else was there. Goya looked at the lovely noblewoman. The lovely noblewoman looked at Goya. They both smiled.

Then the husband went suddenly to the door, walked through, turned around and closed it. And having closed it on Goya and the beautiful young noblewoman alone in the studio he locked the door from the outside.

"This door is going to remain locked until you have painted my wife's portrait!" he called triumphantly. Then he went away.

And sure enough, when he returned at the end of the day he found the door still locked, just as he had left it. He opened the door. Goya was still there, looking remarkably pleased with himself. The beautiful noblewoman was still there, looking charming.

"Well?" said the husband who had thought up a way.

"Oh, there you are!" said the wife who had wanted to be painted by Goya.

[141]

"And there's your portrait," said Goya, who could do one very easily in two hours. A portrait of the lady was drying on the easel.

"I'm glad to see that you have done what I wanted," said the husband who had thought up a way.

"As it turned out, I was very glad to," said Francisco Goya.

Matheron says that Goya saw the beautiful noblewoman a good deal, after that, and Stokes believes she is the heroine of the story about the painted wound. That was on the occasion when her husband was anxious to have her leave Goya's company, rather than remain in it. He had to go to Aranjuez, where the king was holding court. He wanted her to go along.

She wanted to stay in Madrid. "She asked Goya to invent a sufficient excuse. He picked up a brush and painted on her naked foot an appalling bruise. The Marquis"—he was definitely a marquis—"was in despair when his attention was drawn to the wound. He called in a physician. Sangrado examined the injured limb, declared the case one of gravity, and prescribed dressings, bandages, and, above all, the most absolute rest. Very troubled, the Marquis proceeded alone to Aranjuez." She remained in Madrid with Goya. So runs the tale.

VI
The Fair Rewards
[1799–1808]

VI

The Fair Rewards

[1799–1808]

I

At the turn of the century, with his greatest work still
before him, Goya came into the fair rewards. In July, 1799,
San Francisco de la Florida was opened for all Madrid to see
the gayety of his murals, and in October Charles IV made
him first painter to the court, with a salary of 50,000 reales a
year, 500 ducats a year for travel, and the promise of
Maella's house as soon as Maella departed. He was a celebrity and a great success.

"His fame as a portraitist had reached the court," Beruete
observes; "the great ladies and nobles of the period sought
to have their portrait by Goya, and no less the sovereigns of
the royal family." Goya himself expressed his elation spirit-
edly in a letter to Zapater telling him of his appointment and
ending with the Goyesque remark: "Los Reyes estan locos
con tu amigo."

The portraits of that triumphant period are a gallery of
the patricians of Spain. Some of them were so fabulously
wealthy that they could challenge the king in ostentation.
One family was proud of being able to travel all the way to
the French border without leaving its own lands. A legendary nobleman of that day is supposed to have sent a mistress

[145]

who complained of the winter in Madrid a brazier filled with gold coins.

Goya painted their biographies in their faces. The Conde de Fernan Nuñez, standing in a tricorn hat, white stock and dark coat, is the apotheosis of the romantic Spanish ancestor, the inevitable gallant for Goya's painting of the *Majas on the balcony*.

The pretentiousness of the Marques de Bondad Real is in Goya's portrait of him standing on a parade ground, looking inadequate even to the task of drilling the toy soldiers who drill in the background. And dozens of other tailor-made warriors are in the gallery. Goya had, by now, many more commissions than he had the time—or the inclination—to carry out himself. He did not want, in any case, to devote all his days to the manufacture of fashionable portraits. So he got Esteve, a pupil, to help him turn out the swarming hidalgos.

These were the powers of Spain. They were steeped in a feudal tradition that had long since started going to seed. The greatness of Spain was dwindling because they had forgotten how to conquer and could not learn how to rule. Geoffrey Bruun observes that "to the great landowners, jealous of their social and feudal privileges, the French example was anathema. The regular clergy, numerous and richly endowed despite the general poverty of the country, could offer strong opposition to the secularization of their property. The Church and the Inquisition had trained the faithful to regard religious tolerance as little better than heresy and atheism. No large and literate middle class, raised on Rousseau and Montesquieu, clamored for political recognition, and centralizing tendencies in government were not popular in a country where each province clung tenaciously to its peculiar rights." The nobility and the clergy and the throne saw to that, however much they might be divided on other matters in Spain.

Lady Holland has some revealing tales to tell about the grandees of Spain. Indeed, her journal might have been written as a commentary on the portraits Goya painted. It was she who wrote in September, 1803: "The King of Spain is so little *au courant* of the history of our times that he is as yet not aware of the independence of America, and to this day denominates the Minister of the United States *El Ministro de las Colonias*, being perfectly satisfied that these colonies still belong to the English."

In the course of the next year she made many shrewd notations on her impressions of the grandees of Spain. The young Fernan Nuñez, she thought, was a "gentlemanly person, countenance that denotes more sense than he possesses." And the Marquesa de Santiago, one of the more curious portraits in Goya's gallery, was "very profligate and loose in her manners and conversation, and scarcely admitted to female society." Madame de Montijo had "an uncommon share of wit and talent and a satirical bent, which she is apt to indulge at the expense of the Court, for which she has an undisguised contempt and dislike." The rumble of war sounds also in Lady Holland's pages,[1] for she, unlike many of the grandees Goya was painting, was fully aware of the gathering European storm.

[1]*The Spanish Journal of Elizabeth Lady Holland.* Edited by the Earl of Ilchester. Longmans, Green & Co., 1910.

2

IN THE spring of 1800 Goya rode often down the dusty roads through green country to Aranjuez, where the king liked to rest under Philip's English elms.

Aranjuez was always Charles IV's favorite palace. He enjoyed being painted there in the rooms looking out over the water gardens, the island and the Tagus River. As Crown Prince he had designed one of the many gardens. Presently, he was to build himself a fabulously expensive "laborer's cottage" there in the manner of the Petit Trianon, filled with such authentic details of rusticity as mosaics, silver-panelled walls, and quantities of terrible sculpture.

When Goya arrived with his canvases chaos was still in the future. But within the decade Charles was to abdicate at Aranjuez and go into exile with no further need to pretend that he was a simple man with only a small house to live in and no kingdom in Europe or empire strewn around the seven seas. Now he was King of Spain and the Indies, employing all the painters he could find in his kingdom to present him as such to posterity.

The others painted him more suitably than Goya. They and their works are now largely forgotten. Goya painted the king as he saw him, he painted Maria Luisa as he saw her, and her children with equal truth. And this has given them all a somewhat unenviable immortality.

It has, we noted, been a question why Goya could paint those grotesque sovereigns so unflatteringly and remain ungarrotted. He took precisely the opposite position from Velasquez, who gave all his Philips their look of poached nobility.

The answer is that Goya was the leading painter of his day, and many experiences had taught his sitters that they could not teach him how to paint. So Carlos and Maria Luisa were content to be painted by Goya. They did not foresee that history would use his portraits in judging them. They asked him to paint them again and again. And, being Goya, he was popular with them.

That Spring he had gone to Aranjuez to paint a picture of the whole royal family on one enormous canvas. It was a considerable undertaking, with every possibility that the result would be lamentable or simply dull. There were thirteen people to be painted in the group, from a venerable and slightly gastric-looking old princess to a baby who seems to have slept through the whole harrowing proceeding, and just wakened at the end.

Goya painted himself into the picture, standing at his easel at the left, looking a good deal more eminent than life, the one unrealistic portrait in the lot. It has been suggested that he painted his own portrait in the group to break the unlucky number and make a fourteenth. This is an ingenious explanation. But there are too many precedents, in every nation's art, of painters who have put themselves in groups sacred or profane to make us wonder why Goya should have done that here. He had done it before. And is there any doubt that Goya would have painted his own portrait in if he wanted to, whether the family of Charles IV contained twenty members or two?

As autobiography, Goya's portrait of himself is remarkably interesting. He stands aloof from the restless glitter of the royal family that has brought all its regalia to show. In a dark coat with a white stock Goya looks gravely out over their heads, a man interested only in his art's strict discipline. It is easy to believe that he is the foremost painter of his day, it is not so apparent that this is the Goya of the escapades. He has presented the pride without the arrogance; he has presented only one side of himself. Just as he said, when some one showed him his early work in Fuendetodos: "You would not say I had painted that!" so here he seems to be ready to say: "You would not suggest that I intended a satire in this portrait of the royal family!"

That is precisely what the world does say. The painting was in the palace at Madrid at the end of the Napoleonic wars. In the Prado it had the place of honor at the end of the main gallery, which is so long you can almost see the curve of the earth along its floor. Before assembling them all on one canvas Goya made preparatory portraits. He painted only the heads, against his favorite red-brown tierra de Sevilla ground. These were done very quickly at Aranjuez that spring.

The whole family was not at the palace. In his bill for paint and canvas—and carriages—Goya mentioned only ten. The elderly infanta and a slightly younger one seem to have been dropped into v-spaces in the background. The King's brother looks over his shoulder, barely making an appearance, and the medals he wore so proudly for the preparatory sketch do not show at all. But the baby in the arms of the Princess of Parma wears her order of Charles III like a bib. No one knows who all the thirteen are, for two of the older princesses are forever in dispute, faces in a masterpiece of satirical biography.

THE FAMILY OF CHARLES IV

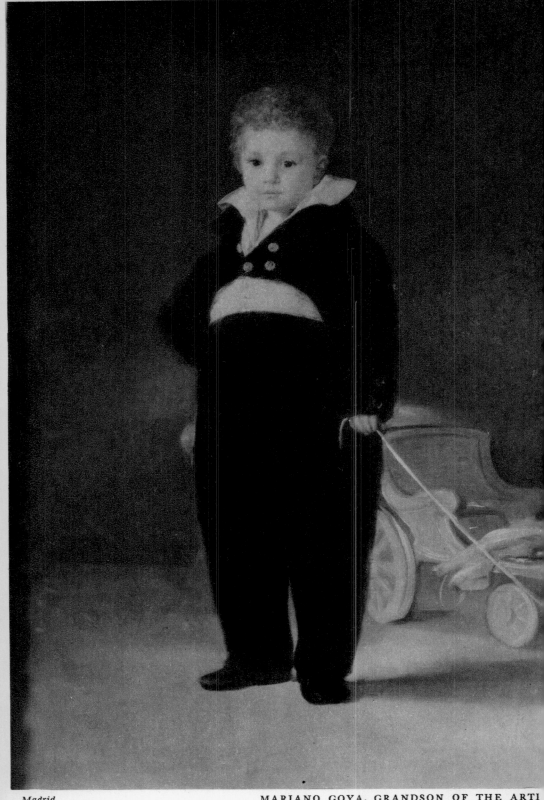

MARIANO GOYA, GRANDSON OF THE ARTI

Beside Ferdinand, the crown prince, a girl stands with her face turned away. Ferdinand's bride had not then been chosen. So Goya made her features indistinct enough to stand for whatever princess he ultimately married. The face of anonymity has its own appropriateness: Ferdinand had four wives before he finally, to the relief of all Spain, died.

Prince Carlos, a boy of ten, stands beside his brother. Carlos was to give his name to the Carlist faction that fought unendingly for the throne. In the center of the picture Queen Maria Luisa stands with one arm on the shoulder of the Infante Francisco de Paula, who has been called her child by Godoy. An immense jewelled arrow is in the Queen's hair, and on her face an expression of harpy malevolence. Beside her, the King stands with all the ribbons and orders of a sovereign, and none of the qualities, fat, futile, cabrón-faced. Gautier's remark: "He looks like a grocer who has just won the big lottery prize, with his family around him," is a more acute observation than its uncharitable tone may suggest.

3

GOYA was popular in the palace, though he had no very high opinion of the King. His free ways of doing what he wanted to do and going where he wanted to go were known to every one in Madrid. Stokes recalls a story about a time when the court was in mourning and Goya arrived at the palace wearing white stockings and white knee breeches. The guards stopped him. The royal chamberlain said he could not appear in that costume.

"All right," said Goya, "I'll change the costume." Then,

according to the tale, he proceeded to draw caricatures of the chamberlain and the guards all over the stockings. For a moment they were speechless. And in that moment Goya went past them to the King, who was very glad to see him, particularly as a walking cartoon.

On one occasion the King played his violin for Goya. In a letter to Zapater Goya spoke of that, without comment on the fact that it was odd to think of the King playing for a man who was deaf. It must have been a strange scene.

Charles IV liked to play the violin, but the court chronicles do not venture to suggest that he was good at it. Indeed, they say that when he took part in a quartet an abler musician stood behind a screen to play the King's share resonantly enough to drown out his scrapings.

Goya enjoyed music so much that in the years of exile when he was completely deaf he still plucked at a guitar for the pleasure it gave him. And he sent Zapater the latest pieces, telling him to copy them and not tell any one where he got them.

There is nothing about the quality of the King's music in Goya's letter to Zapater. He only speaks of it incidentally in the course of mentioning various things that happened at the palace: "I went to see the King today, and he received me very cheerfully, speaking of my Paco's[1] smallpox (which he knew about) so I gave him an account of it and he gave me his hand and began to play the violin." Then Goya goes on to say that he had approached the King wondering what would happen, since his enemies had been telling the King

---

[1]His son, Francisco Javier, the only one of Goya's twenty children who survived him.

that Goya did not want to paint for him. The palace cama-
rillas were always busy developing their plots.

Yet Goya painted a good many portraits for the King and
Queen in those years. Maria Luisa was particularly pleased
with the portrait of herself riding Marcial, the vast horse
Godoy had given her. That was painted the year before the
family portrait, and she wrote Godoy from the Escorial,
where Goya had gone to do the picture, that it was finished
in three sittings, and "they tell me it is an even better likeness than the one with the mantilla."[1] It is decidedly a less
unflattering portrait than the cackling likeness in the mantilla. Riding Marcial in the uniform of a Colonel of the
Guards, astride, Maria Luisa has a certain imperious stature.
The face may have been done in three sittings, painting the
horse must have taken a little longer; it looks like a stallion
from the Velasquezan stable crossed with the horse in Titian's
incomparable portrait of Charles V. Yet it seems to have been
regarded as a good portrait of Marcial. Goya had better success here than he often had in painting horses outside the
bullring. On the whole, only his plaza de toros horses are
completely convincing. There is usually the suggestion of
a touch of flounder blood in his stallions. More epic than
hippic, many of them belong with the other strange beasts
of Goya's mythology.

Goya went from Aranjuez to Madrid, out to the monastic
Escorial—which looks remarkably like an American peniten-
tiary, if one forgets its imperial history—and back to the
pleasures of Madrid. In August he wrote Zapater that he

---

[1]*Cartas Confidenciales de La Reina Maria Luisa y de Don Manuel Godoy.* Carlos
Pereyra. Madrid.

was doing the sketch of Godoy on horseback. By the time the portrait was completed, Godoy had dismounted. He appears as a marshal in the field, sitting his fat bulk on one rock and leaning on another, reading a dispatch held at arm's length, an aide at his shoulder and a plumed hat and sword beside him while he holds a stick between his knees. Almost the White Knight. The horses stand just behind Godoy: Goya painted the nearest one to him facing the other way. Godoy's principal military exploit was the preposterous expedition against Portugal. It is called the War of the Oranges, for the branch he sent Maria Luisa from the unarduous campaign.

It was a relief to be asked to paint Godoy's wife. Goya had known her and liked her a long time, ever since the days at Arenas, when he had painted her in her father's house as a child. Her father was the unfrocked Infante, Don Luis, who had lost his royal rank when he married, as we said, the lady from Aragon. This daughter, light-haired and trusting and young, had been forced to marry Godoy, though he was the Queen's lover and though he had another mistress, Pepita Tudo. In that way Godoy became a relative of the royal family, and it was hoped that some of the scandal would be silenced, as well.

4

BULLFIGHTING flourished vastly between 1789—when Charles IV celebrated his accession to the throne with a resplendent *corrida* in Madrid—and 1805, when he decided to abolish that frequently abolished sport. Charles IV's decision to put an end to bullfighting was taken on the ground that it was bad for the humanitarian reputation of Spain, bad for agriculture, in that it diverted too much land and effort to the raising of bulls, and bad for the people who should, he had been persuaded, be at work rather than at the bullring.

Before Charles IV came to those belated conclusions, however, Spanish bullfighting completed one of its most celebrated periods. It was a time, as Ángel Salcedo Ruiz observes, when the tradition of the famous Ronda school of bullfighting, founded by Francisco Romero (the first, it is said, to kill with the muleta) was ably carried on by his successors. One of these successors was Romero's son, Juan, who lived to be 102, and in turn left a bullfighting son, Pedro, born half a dozen years after Goya.

The Sevillan school was represented by Costillares (whose real name was Pedro Joaquín Rodríguez) and José Delgado, known as Pepe-Hillo. There were other bullfighters, followers of one school or the other: Cándido, Chiclanero, Curro-Guillén among them. But the three in the top flight were Romero, Costillares and Pepe-Hillo. These three, according to Ángel Salcedo Ruiz, were paid about 3000 pesetas for each fight, which was a double one, or held half in the morning and half in the afternoon. But they did not have to pay for their *cuadrillas*. The impresario did that, giving a good picador 800 *reales*, a good *banderillero* 400.

The most popular bullfighter of the day was Pepe-Hillo. His skill in the ring was as celebrated as his skill with the ladies. And when Pepe-Hillo was killed in Madrid, in 1801, the tragedy caused national lamentation. Even the name of the bull that killed him—Barbudo—became historic.

Goya immortalized the episode of Pepe-Hillo's death in

the thirty-third plate of the *Tauromaquia*. He may have made the etching from a drawing done at the time of the cornada. The etching itself was probably completed some time later, a part of Goya's historic record of bullfighting in Spain.

It was in those days of egalitarianism blown by the winds of the French Revolution that bullfighting changed from a pastime that was exclusively the right of the nobles to a popular, democratic sport. Then, for the first time, the nobility began, reluctantly, to share with the people the privilege of being gored and having their internal economy strewn around the ring.

Goya showed that, in his etchings. He showed how in the olden days it was heroes like the Cid and kings like Charles V who went out and risked their lives for the pleasure and skill and excitement of it.

In the old days bullfights had been put on as spectacles on great occasions, such as the coronation of a new monarch. That custom remained. But in place of the monarchs getting out in the Plaza Mayor under the cape-decorated balconies, it was the professionals.

And as Goya's art shows, every town had its bullring, or fought the bulls down streets that held Spain's first barricades.

He signed himself "Francisco de los Toros." He is supposed, as we know, to have gone to Rome as a member of a bullfighter's cuadrilla. He told Moratin at Bordeaux: "I used to be a bullfighter in my youth, and with the sword in hand I feared nothing." He wrote Zapater: "Monday I am going to the bullfight, God willing, and I wish you were going with me." He painted Pepe-Hillo, Costillares and Romero, the great bullfighters of his time. Truth and legend indissolubly one, it seems clear that Goya enjoyed bullfighting. Not even the most pious biographer, wanting, as all biographers don't, to tamper with destiny and change the record here and there in a subject's life, can change that interest in Goya.

Long before he made the *Tauromaquía* or the famous lithographs called *Los Toros de Burdeos*, Goya had painted many bullfighting scenes. The tapestry cartoons are witness to that. One shows the town gallants practicing with a rather genial bull (who alone is not interested in the fact that he is being painted). Another shows picadors with the ladies who share their principal interest. Another one shows the children playing—as we said—with the wickerwork effigy of a bull borne on one child's head while the others take their turns as toreros.

The double bullring was a custom of the time. It was a familiar spectacle to Spaniards, though foreign visitors noted it with surprise. Lady Holland—who like many English-speaking visitors since, went to bullfights the better to be able to say she did not approve of them—wrote in 1803 that "for the last three bulls the arena was divided by a high fence of wooden paling, which enabled them to regale the public with two *fiestas* or *corridas* at once; those animals were very furious, several horses were killed, and the *picadores* thrown. The only extra accident was the tossing of a poor fellow, whose eagerness carried him into the arena to see the bull come forth, who, instead of attacking the *picador*, attacked and threw him over his horns with the utmost violence."[1]

[1]*Lady Holland's Spanish Journal.*

5

NOWHERE does the greatness of Goya as an artist and as an incomparable historian of Spain and Spanish life come out with more memorable effectiveness than in his drawings. These have yet to be presented as a whole to the world. The infinite riches of the Prado collection are suggested in the rare "Cien Dibujos Inéditos" of Boix and Sánchez Cantón, and one hopes that some day the magnificent collection from the Madrazo Album acquired by the Metropolitan Museum of Art in New York in 1936 will appear in book form.[1] It was in a note on one of the drawings from the Madrazo Album that Harry B. Wehle observed that "The comparison of the drawings of Goya with those of Rembrandt does honor to both artists."

And again, under the drawing of the two prisoners in irons, Mr. Wehle said: "Goya's drawings of prisoners are bloodcurdling in their realization of intense suffering and stupefying misery. His inscriptions on some of these works reveal an excruciating sympathy and a reformer's intention."

That is true. In the Prado drawings there are many searing commentaries on the sufferings of victims of brutal penalties fixed by the throne or the Inquisition. Here is a man stretched on the rack. Why? "Because he discovered the movement of the earth," Goya noted. A woman is in the stocks for showing sympathy to the Liberal cause. A girl, wearing the Inquisition's dunce cap, is there "For having been born in another part."

[1] One's hopes have been realized. "Fifty Drawings by Francisco Goya" has just been published by the Metropolitan with a fine commentary by Mr. Wehle.

In the prison scenes Goya sketched a man being tortured in a cell: "It is better to die." There is a sketch of a man being garrotted—a form of death Ferdinand found a peculiarly appealing instrument of government. "Many end thus," is Goya's comment—a comment that might have cost him his own life if it had come to the eyes of Ferdinand's *camarilla* in the days of that sovereign's white terror. And under a drawing of a man being flogged to death: "He has not yet died."

These drawings have an exceptionally wide range. Sometimes Goya draws the fantastic visions of his nightmares. Again, he shows a horned man: "He says that he's had them since he was born." A sketch of an old man with his arms around a young girl is sardonically titled: "Paternal embrace." And the priest riding on the back of a worker with a hoe needs no explanation. The picture of a bound man, about to be hoisted, while friars stand by, is called: "Do you conform?"

Under a sketch of a frantic man in what seems to be the last stages of distraction, Goya wrote: "This one has many relatives—and some are rational." Under a sketch of a Diogenes figure with a lantern: "You won't find him." And in a sketch that most certainly represents himself as an incredibly old man who needs two sticks to support him, wearing a long white symbolic beard—Goya never had one—he wrote: "Aún aprendo"—"I'm still learning."

"Divina razón," he wrote under a sketch of Justice flogging away the dark birds of reaction, "no deges ninguno" —"Divine reason, don't spare one of them." Looking at that one thinks again of Ferdinand's epoch.

[159]

There are sketches that prophesy paintings and etchings Goya made later on. The dancing crowd of Madrileños celebrating the verbena of the *Entierro de la Sardina*, for example, or the somber vision of *El Sueño de la Razón*—"The Dream of Reason"—with Goya's face among the supernal bat figures, once meant, undoubtedly, for the frontispiece of the *Caprichos*.

The drawing of the three laborers swinging mattocks in a field (in the Metropolitan collection) is, as Mr. Wehle has pointed out, very similar in composition to the painting of the men at the forge that now hangs in the Frick collection. The unlocking of the conspicuously padlocked women is in a more sardonic mood.

6

SOME of the drawings are hilarious, and more than one is Rabelaisian. In the Metropolitan collection there is the episode of the dire, clinical and painful revenge taken upon an unfortunate constable. In the Prado, there is a double drawing showing a girl fully dressed on one side—and decidedly not dressed at all, on the other.

Goya's intense interest in the bullring is shown again in the huge collection of red-chalk drawings of *toreros* in action he made, perhaps for his own amusement in the first place, as records of *corridas* he had seen or heard about, and that he used later on for the *Tauromaquia*.

Since Goya was forever sketching it is not surprising that the dating of his drawings presents many problems that seem insoluble. They are not always as inscrutable as they appear to some observers, however. Just as the Egyptian carving on the chair of Goya's portrait of Doña Teresa Sureda (wife of the young tosspot in the companion portrait) should suggest that at least it must have been painted after Bonaparte's Egyptian campaign, so the drawings have their own inferential data. Indeed, it may be plainer than that. I remember showing Enrique LaFuente of the Biblioteca—who knows as much about Goya's etchings and drawings as any one else this side of Paradise—a copy of a Goya drawing that turned up in London (it brought 500 guineas, having been bought in 1921 for 70 pounds) in the Summer of 1936. It was stated that the drawing was thought to be contemporaneous with the time of the *Desastres*. Whereupon he pointed out that was scarcely reasonable, since the date "Junio . . . 1799" was plainly written beneath the wash of the "cave" the drawing concerned.

The fifty drawings at the Metropolitan may very well, as Mr. Wehle suggests, belong to three different periods. Certainly the early ones recall the days of Sanlúcar, and the face that always haunted Goya's work is there in its unmistakable loveliness. The girl in the swing wears a dress that is a little like the dress the Duchess of Alba wore in the imperious portrait of the two rings at the Hispanic. And this drawing also foretells the Alameda painting—very much in the manner of a tapestry cartoon—made for the Osunas in 1787, in our day protected for some time at the Madrid palace of the Duke of Montellano. An interesting self-portrait, rather on the Directoire side, is a part of the album. And in the later sketches—particularly the one Mr. Wehle calls "Truth Beset by Dark Spirits"—events of the years when Ferdinand was crushing, with unexampled brutality, the liberalism of the Constitution of Cadiz, are clearly in Goya's mind.

The gossip of the day no less than the issues of the epoch appear in Goya's drawings, whether they are scrawled in nervous pencilled notations or done in india ink, sepia, or colored chalk. The episode of the infuriated women who killed the Alguacil Lampiños with a douche of quicklime for persecuting students and women of fortune must have been the talk of the town. The drawing called "The Tantrum," showing a woman tearing her hair angrily while a periwigged man stands by with his back turned carries the explanation: "She orders them to leave the coach, tears her hair and stamps her foot, all because the Abbé Pichurris told her she lacked color," may be based on a quarrel in the course of the journey to Sanlúcar. For again the girl in the drawing reminds you of the Duchess of Alba.

The man pouring himself full from a wineskin while a woman remonstrates and tries to make him stop is simply called: "Later you'll see." A more convivial drinking scene shows four women and a man rapidly emptying a somewhat inadequate bottle. And later on there is another man with another wineskin. He can no longer stand, but he can still pour.

Goya turned easily from the profane to the sacred; indeed he often mixed them up while he was about it. He drew a prelate balancing perilously on a slack rope while an immense crowd looks on. He dropped his more usual acerbity toward friars, as Sanchez Canton and Boix have observed, in the rear view of a friar half drowned in robes ("Cuantas baras?") and in the sketch of the two shirtless ones, "Sin camisa son felices."

The girls of this world and the witches of the other were never far from Goya's mind, and one is never long without them in his drawings—or anything else that he did, for that matter. Sometimes he drew in a single sketch the best and the worst of both worlds—as in the Prado's red chalk drawing of the naked girl, her hair streaming in the wind, riding through the air on the back of the Great Goat himself, while beneath them two *brujas* pilot the way toward whatever gathering waits their coming.

7

GODOY's foreign policies added materially to the damages his internal policies caused Spain. He led the country into war with France during the first half of the seventeen nineties; during the second half he was allied with France against England. At the end of his first war he was given the title of Prince of the Peace for his settlement at Basle; his statesmanship at the end of the second manœuvre was not so heartily admired, and, in 1798, he was thrown out by what might be called popular acclamation.

Since he had never enjoyed the admiration of the people and never would, Godoy's main problem was to get back into the good graces of Maria Luisa, who is said to have been displeased by his incontinence toward Spain and infuriated by his incontinence toward her. When he had accomplished that he was secure; when he attracted the attention of Napoleon he was launched as a statesman again. He aspired to military glory, and so, in the process of carrying out a chore for Napoleon, he invaded Portugal. This, as we noted, was the preposterous War of the Oranges.

Under Godoy, the humiliation of Spain at the hands of Napoleon proceeded at a brisk tempo. Louisiana, which had been ceded to France in 1800, was sold by Napoleon to the United States in order to raise money to fight England. Spain, which had recently owned Louisiana, and felt a little sulky at the sale, was called upon to share in Napoleon's plan to invade British shores. This presently led to the most famous of all the defeats of the period, when Nelson triumphed at Trafalgar.

The greater catastrophe was not far away. Ferdinand, heir to the throne, had begun to intrigue on his own account. It may be, as some historians believe, that he was in fear of being cut out of the succession by Godoy and Maria Luisa. It is certain, in any case, that his communication with Napoleon was treason to his father and mother. Ferdinand was exposed and forgiven.

The increasing number of Napoleonic troops in Spain should have warned them all that they could never hope to save themselves through the emperor. Yet greater than their fear of Napoleon was their hatred of one another. Ferdinand and Godoy despised each other heartily; Ferdinand was on poor terms with his father and in open hostility toward his mother, who returned the sentiment. Charles IV bumbled around uncertainly, threatening, cajoling, trying to keep the peace where there was no peace to be had. Ferdinand's repentance after he was exposed in the Escorial conspiracy did not last long. Under the influence of his old tutor, Canon Escoïquiz, he went on plotting to seize the throne.

In justice to Godoy it should be said that he alone among those in the palace spoke of opposing Napoleon with arms.

But that was widely regarded as lunacy. Instead, the king and queen decided that the only thing to do was to run for their lives, as the royal family of Portugal had done when they went to Brazil. The plan was to be carried out with no public announcement. But when the court moved to Aranjuez, as the first step on a journey that was planned to take them next to Seville and then, possibly, to America, a popular uprising—skillfully staged by the adherents of Ferdinand—threw all plans into chaos.

The people (led by Ferdinand's provocators) clamored around the king's palace, demanding that Godoy be given over to them. When they were told that Godoy was about to make his escape they broke into the house occupied by that Prince of the Peace in furious search of him. His mistress, Pepita Tudo, was safe; his wife—the tragic daughter of the Infante Don Luis—was not hurt, but the rooms were wrecked. The crowd, coached to do so, shouted vengeance on Godoy and demanded that Ferdinand be made king.

VII

The War's Disasters

[1808–1814]

VII

The War's Disasters

[1808–1814]

I

GOYA was living in the Puerta del Sol in the spring of
1808. His own life was comparatively tranquil. Around him
Madrid seethed with daily sensations, from the echoing palace to the lowest steps in Lavapies.

He was aware of what momentous events went on. Charles
IV, more muddled than ever, had been forced to resign, the
increasingly paunchy Godoy, who had been found hiding in
a rug at Aranjuez, was in terror for his life, and Ferdinand
was king. But the day before Ferdinand entered Madrid as
sovereign, Murat had marched in at the head of Napoleon's
men. And Murat joined in none of the ovations that thousands of Spaniards—who were to need more seeing of Ferdinand in action to realize what a scoundrel he was—gave him.
Napoleon was no more interested in recognizing Ferdinand
than he was in having his father stay on the throne. He had
other plans for Spain.

For while Charles IV was solemnly stalking rabbits in the
Casa de Campo, Napoleon had been speculatively pointing a
gun at him. An easy kill. After studying him some time,
Napoleon cocked his gun. But, amazingly, Carlos started to
run, and after running around in circles for a little while,
he ran straight to Napoleon.

The soldiers of Napoleon marched into Madrid under Goya's windows. Some of them were young recruits with the apron strings of Normandy still marking their wrists. Many were old campaigners who had not for years on end understood the languages of the men they killed.

Murat occupied the coronada villa. And though Charles IV had abdicated in favor of his son, the son was not honored as king by the invaders. Murat himself hoped to be king under the talons of the eagles. Napoleon had other plans for the throne of Spain. But Murat knew that the whole Bourbon family was to be dispossessed by the strength of the same land that had put them there.

The people of Madrid were uneasy at first, and, gradually, furious. Out of simple-hearted loyalty they were ready to defend their own—even when their own was one so stained and chilling to the heart as Ferdinand. They were ready to stand and fight for their king. You could not say that such heroism was the last thing in the minds of Charles IV and Ferdinand VII; it was not in their minds at all. They had no intention of fighting. And they did not fight, for the simple reason that there was no fight in them.

Napoleon was going south through France. In Madrid the story was told that he would soon be on his way through Castile to see the king. A long row of rooms along one of the endless corridors of the palace was swept and dusted and decorated for him, piled luggage marked for the Emperor was unloaded with public show, there were those who had seen his hat and his boots arrive. Which king of Spain was Napoleon going to see? Murat treated the confused and bumbling Charles IV as king. In name, Ferdinand reigned.

Goya had been asked to paint Ferdinand's portrait by weathervane courtiers. He did it very quickly, with splashes of color for the uniform and an apparent lack of admiration for the clenched, suspicious face.

Goya's portraits of Ferdinand could be repeated in any variety. He had devised the way. If you look at the standing figures of Ferdinand Goya painted you will see that he has one arm bent at his side, the other slightly extended. That is the cut-out, for all the world like a child's paper doll. The dress can be changed. And Goya changed it, to show Ferdinand wearing the robes of a king or the uniform of a soldier, holding a sword or a baton. The half-length pictures take just half as much trouble. When Ferdinand appears on horseback, it is as though he had been bent into position. But the expression of liverish grimness, the mouth like a stitched tear, never changes.

2

MADRID rose against Napoleon the night before the second of May. In the rookeries down around Lavapies no one went to sleep. Groups stood on every corner. They cursed the name of Napoleon. They did not care what happened to the Queen of Etruria—she was an *afrancesada*. She would be better off in France. That was where she belonged. Good riddance. Let her go. But they would not let the Napoleonic soldiers take away the last young prince. He must remain in Madrid. How could they prevent Murat's men from taking him? What could they do against the thousands and thousands of crack troops Napoleon had in Madrid? Those questions did not stop the Madrileños. Their own troops were useless, their own leaders had failed them. They would take matters into their own hands.

Through the shadows they swarmed toward the enormous palace. It was a Bastille. There it loomed, high over the Manzanares, impregnable. It was held by troops of a man who had got his start when the Bastille was taken by just such a determined expression of the will of the people. They stood there, packed deep, looking up at the high windows set in granite. By daylight the square was jammed. It was jammed with the people of Madrid. Not the periwigged grandees of Spain with all their illustrious titles and memories of brave ancestors safely dead. These stayed in their houses and curried the favor of the French. It was the anonymous poor, the people who made Madrid, who did its work and got nothing for it, who were there to protect the son of the king.

Nine o'clock in the morning. From the enormous royal stables below the palace three ornate carriages drove up to the gates. One, the people heard, was for the Queen of Etruria and her children. Let her go. She went. The others were for Don Antonio, who was the weak head of the weak junta, and for the young Francisco de Paula. This Infante, the people heard, was in the palace, and he was crying. He did not want to go away. He was being forced to go by Napoleon's men. They were about to lay hands on him and carry him away from Spain.

That set the blaze. The crowd began to shout, to storm, to move. An aide of Murat's appeared. Here was a symbol of the force that was oppressing them, of the *gabachos*, the invaders. All the fury in the crowd centered on him, and on the soldiers who rode with him. The Madrileños would have torn him to bits, and his escort, and the Spanish Walloon guards that appeared next, and the French troops that came after. The people of Madrid were bent on seeing that the young Infante was not kidnapped. They got to the carriage, cut the traces, took the horses away.

Murat sent more troops to slaughter them. Cannon and rifle fire were trained on the people of Madrid. The French shelled them mercilessly. They had the guns, and the people of Madrid had not. Men and women began to fall, wounded or dead. But that did not change the spirit of the town. Instead of putting down a riot the French had started the Spanish War of Independence.

If you are standing in a street with nothing but a stick or a knife in your hand you cannot do much against cannon. The cannon is eminently superior. It is a shining, large-scale, scientific instrument, meant to kill many citizens at once, which makes it superior to the knife or the stick. But in Madrid the people with the knives and the sticks believed in their cause with a desperate heroism. The cannon could not stop them. They rushed at the blond cavalrymen from Poland, the dark mameluke cavalry from Egypt, and these could not stop the people of Madrid either.

Murat sent for more guns. He ordered more cavalry charges against the people who had come out of their houses. Practically unarmed, wholly untrained citizens, who were accustomed only to carry heavy loads for the nobility, or sweep floors for them, or carry water, or cut wood or work in shops, making shoes and candles and things like that. But very Spanish, very brave.

The streets were running blood, now. You can see what the

fighting was like in the Puerta del Sol on the second of May if you look at Goya's painting of the scene.

The nobility stayed indoors, and wondered what was to become of law and order if people got to disobeying the cannon of Napoleon this way. "With very few exceptions," Hume remarks, "the nobles, officials, civil and military, and the higher classes generally, either stood aloof, or effusively rallied to the foreign intruder. But base as was the conduct of the ruling elements in Spain in the supreme moment of national history, it was dignified and patriotic in comparison with the behavior of the royal family in Bayonne." And it was for that royal family that the people of Madrid were dying.

The people had been fighting through the morning without organization, without any other idea than to hold the prince who was being taken away from them. Their fury embodied the pent-up desperation against the brutal taking over of Madrid by Napoleon's men. There were in the town people who might have led them. But these were making themselves scarce. Until Daoiz and Velarde by taking command of the spontaneous uprising made themselves immortal. Velarde, a captain of artillery, unlike his fellow officers, was on the people's side. He led them to the barracks, where French and Spanish troops were in charge. The junta had ordered them not to join the uprising. But under the goad of Velarde's words they came out for the people. Daoiz, the commander at the barracks, led them.

The people were armed, now. Guns were passed out to the people as they were on the 18th of July, 1936. And they prepared to make their stand. All day they fought. They were fighting in a hopeless battle, but not in a hopeless cause. By their valor they stirred Spain to resist Napoleon. It was to take five years to drive him out. And there were moments when the cause grew even more hopeless than on the Dos de Mayo. But the opposition to him, which was dramatized in Madrid on the second of May—the Dos de Mayo—never ended. It is preposterous to call that a revolt; it was opposition to domination by an invader. It was their own houses they were defending. Their own town. Their own Spain.

The most tragic part of it all was that they were fighting for their own king, Fernando, by general agreement one of the most contemptible men who ever sat on a throne. It was with the cry: "Viva Fernando!" that they stood beside what guns they had, with not much ammunition, and fought as they had sworn to fight, till they were nearly all dead. Civilians, women, loading those smoking guns and firing them while the French came on and on, inexhaustible in their greater numbers, better equipment, trained leadership. Napoleon's men were thrown back again and again. They had less stomach for the battle than the Spaniards. It was not their houses or their daughters or their wives they were fighting for. The French, indeed, had enough of it first, for all their superior numbers and better cannon. Their commander, Lagrange, put up a white flag and suggested talking terms. Daoiz went out to meet him, though he had already been hit. They started to talk. Then, as Hume says, they started to quarrel, and Daoiz was better there. Whereupon the grenadiers bayonetted him to death. And in the confusion the troops of Napoleon filled the fort and butchered all they could lay hands on.

3

THEN the bloody reprisals began. Though the Junta had told the people it was all over, it was not. All over Madrid citizens were shot. It did not matter whether they had even taken part in the resistance. Any pretext was enough for the slaughter. If a man had a pocket knife, he was lined up and shot for bearing arms. Hume says a pair of scissors was used as a reason for the death sentence under Grouchy.

All night long the butchery went on. If you want to see what those firing squads were like, look at Goya's great painting of the scene on the hill where many were executed.

Goya's gardener—Gomez de la Serna says—who was in charge of the Quinta del Sordo in Trueba's time, speaks of those paintings in which "the bullets whistle, the blood gushes, and one hears the cries of the dying."

Trueba puts down the words of the old servant of Goya in this way:

"Have you seen, Señor Isidro said to us, those horrors of war that my poor master painted so admirably? Well I remember the campaign that clamored in the Florida that day and that night, how in the morning my master, mad with indignation, conceived the idea of painting those horrors. From this window he saw the fusillades of the hill of the Prince of Peace, with a gun in his right hand and a blunderbuss loaded with ball shot in the other. If the Frenchmen had started to come here my master and I would have been counterparts of Daoiz and Velarde. Toward midnight my master said to me: Isidro, take your gun and come with me. I obeyed him, and where do you think we went? Why, to the hill, where the poor dead were still unburied. I remember it all as though it had happened yesterday. It was a moonlight night, but since the sky was full of dark clouds, no sooner was there light than there was darkness again. My hair stood on end when I saw my master, with the portfolio in one hand and the gun in the other, turn toward the dead. When my master noticed that all was not well with me he asked:

" 'Dost thou tremble, Othello?' "

"And instead of saying 'I'll tremble myself into a fit,' I nearly burst out crying, thinking that my poor master had gone crazy, because he called me Othello instead of Isidro.

"We sat down on a hillock at whose foot were the dead, my master opened his portfolio, put it on his knees, and waited for the moon to pass a cloud that darkened it. Below the hillock something fluttered, groaned and cried. I—I confess it to you—trembled like quicksilver; but my master went serenely on preparing his paper and pencil between flashes of moonlight. Finally the moon shone as though it were day. In pools of blood we saw a pile of dead bodies, some face down, others face up, this one in the posture of one who kneeling kisses the ground, that one with his hands raised to the sky praying vengeance or mercy—and some hungry dogs were feeding on the dead, growling at the birds of prey that circled over them, wanting to dispute the carcasses they had won!

"While I looked at that picture of horror my master drew it.

"We returned to the house, and the next morning my master showed me his first print of the war, which I, horrified, examined.

" 'Señor'—I asked him—'why do you paint these barbarities of men?'

" 'To have the pleasure'—he answered—'of saying eternally to men that they stop being barbarians.' "

4

GOYA painted what he saw. There is a legend that his first picture of the Dos de Mayo was done on a bullet-printed wall with a rag soaked in the stream of earth and water and Spanish blood, a sketch made savagely on the day of the fighting. But the sketches for the *Desastres* show how thoroughly he recorded the episodes of battle. The sketch in color for the great Dos de Mayo painting and the final life-size scene in the Puerta del Sol are based on these.

What he had seen he painted. Men lie dead under the plunging horses. The soldier on the left is flat and dead on a ground strewn with dropped bayonets, swords, curved sabers. A swung blade has landed under his chin. The man in the center is stabbing the mameluke, who has been yanked backward on his white horse. The mameluke's red trousers do not quite match the color of the blood that streams down his face, and in another minute his gold sash and his blue jacket will be under the hooves of the horses. A Spaniard with a short lance tries in desperation to save two of his comrades on the ground.

Three mamelukes are in the center. One is the dead man. Above him, on the defense, another plunges a dagger at a Madrileño with a Goyesque face. The third, at the back, is still momentarily master of the battle, his scimitar raised.

From those high looming buildings of the Puerta del Sol in the background the people of Madrid are pouring out.

THE DOS DE MAYO

The crowd surges in. Look at those tense and shouting faces. "Mueran los mamelucos!" And on the far right the gold-helmeted officer of Napoleon slashing, the mameluke with his back turned, the Spaniard with a carbine at point blank. All this Goya saw, and when Spaniards think of the Dos de Mayo they remember it through the eyes of Goya.

The fight in the streets of Madrid on the Dos de Mayo was a turning point of tremendous importance to the fortunes of Napoleon. It was the fight that roused the people of every province, from Catalonia to Andalusia. From then on Napoleon was not fighting an army. The army was puny. He was not fighting a dynasty. The dynasty was rotten. He was fighting the peasants from the fields and the charcoal burners from the hills, the cobblers and bakers and winesellers of the towns. He was fighting the people of Spain, and they did not stop fighting for five years: until Napoleon had been whipped out of the peninsula. Many invaders in modern times have got temporary footholds in Spain. But in the end the people have driven them out.

Goya's painting of the Dos de Mayo marks the moment when Napoleon's power began to wane. He said afterwards, at St. Helena, that he never should have gone into Spain at all. Yet it is hard to see how he could have avoided it. He did not, however, count on the nation in arms opposing him. He would have been damned if he had not tried to get Spain. And when he failed to hold Spain, he *was* damned.

5

NAPOLEON did not go to Madrid that spring. He stayed on the French side of the border, at Bayonne. Charles IV

was invited to go and see him there. It was an invitation
with the force of a command. Charles IV was aware of that.
Some of his advisers told him it would be injudicious to leave
his own country. But Charles IV was anxious to see Napoleon and put his case before the Emperor, a father rushing
ingloriously to tattle and complain about his disgraceful son.
So, with a retinue riding uneasily in shabby royal carriages
that looked old-fashioned on French roads, he crossed the
Bidassoa and went to his fate at Bayonne.

It was a hysterical and absurd and rather contemptible
business all around, that meeting at Bayonne. No one concerned came out of it with much honor.

To Charles IV and Maria Luisa the journey to Bayonne
was a last hope. They had already tried once to run out of the
country, but they had been turned back. Now the puppet
master dangled them from one string while he manipulated
Ferdinand with another. Charles had taken back his abdica-
tion and Ferdinand was being given hope that his prayer—
to marry any one of Napoleon's relatives who might be
offered—would be granted.

It was not all, perhaps, quite so simple a resolution as Duff
Cooper suggests when he says that while promising Ferdinand a Bonaparte princess Napoleon "continued to negoti-
ate with the king and queen and arranged for them, together with Godoy, to meet him at Bayonne, with a view to
settling all their differences. To persuade Ferdinand also to
cross the frontier proved only slightly more difficult, although the Spanish people, more perspicacious than their
prince, sought in vain to detain him and actually removed
the horses from his carriage. On his arrival at Bayonne Ferdi-

nand was informed that he must immediately abdicate, and when he refused to do so he was threatened with a trial for high treason. He agreed, in terror, to sign a document restoring the throne to his father and subsequently learnt that his father had already made over all his rights to Napoleon. The miserable old couple were allowed to depart first for Compiègne and then to Italy, where they spent the remainder of their days in universal contempt, but Ferdinand, together with his younger brother and his uncle, was sent to gilded captivity at Talleyrand's château of Valençay."[1] Yet that is a true epitome.

Sencourt's researches show how astonishingly they all behaved. They screamed, they ranted, they completely forgot themselves. Maria Luisa—wearing a yellow dress she had borrowed from the Empress Josephine—was alternately a frantic mother and an indignant sovereign. Neither rôle seems to have fitted her much better than the gown of yellow. It was Ferdinand who got to Bayonne first. But that did not do him any good. Josephine was very nice to the Queen, Napoleon was very nice to the King, they were both very nice to Carlos. And very firm with Ferdinand. They would not have any of him. They ranted around in the scene before Napoleon. The Queen and the King berated their son. Napoleon got Carlos to sign his rights over to him. That was easy. Then the King told Ferdinand he also must abdicate. That was not so simple. But he was finally convinced. The King and Queen went into exile in France, then on to Rome, where they lived with their beloved Manuel. Ferdinand went to Talleyrand's Valençay—but unfortunately, he came back.

[1] *Talleyrand,* by Duff Cooper. Harper & Brothers.

6

GOYA went to Zaragoza in October, travelling through a war-torn country between the sieges. He entered the city, and saw what the siege had done. He heard about the valiant maid of Zaragoza, whose name rang through loyalist Spain.

He went back into the burnt hills, past the Roman ruins and the traces of other invaders, the Moors, who, these too, like Napoleon's men, thought they could conquer Spain. He went back to his native village, to Fuendetodos.

Zapater says there were still people, years later, who recalled that visit. Again we recall that return:

They said Goya, stone deaf, talked through the signs of a hand alphabet. They knew his fame in Madrid. They showed him his retablo. He looked at it wonderingly. He neither accepted it nor declined authorship.

"You wouldn't say I had painted that!"

An unexpected commentary on Goya's journey to Zaragoza between the sieges is in Lady Holland's Journal for April, 1809: "The *artillera*," she writes, referring to the illustrious Augustina of Aragon, "was killed in the 2nd siege by a cannon ball, as were 3 other women who had been inspired by her courage and followed her example. Palafox was insulted by the French and cruelly treated; they removed the surgeon who attended him, and placed a Frenchman in his place. In his room there were several drawings done by the celebrated Goya, who had gone from Madrid on purpose to see the ruins of Saragossa; these drawings and one from the famous heroine above mentioned, also by Goya, the French officers cut and destroyed with their sabres, at the moment too when Palafox was dying in his bed."

Napoleon's men were able to destroy the drawings Goya made more easily than they could destroy the idea; in due course Augustina took her place in the *Desastres de la Guerra*, and the portrait of Palafox—riding that improbable horse— was another memorial of the journey to Zaragoza.

When the military leaders deserted them it was the people of Zaragoza, like the people of Madrid, who seized what arms they could and defended their city with historic valor. The young aristocrat, Palafox, who rallied the people to re- sist Napoleon, was not the only leader. Two men of no such patrician origin, Tio Martín and Tio Jorge, led the people of Zaragoza while Palafox was away, at the beginning of the siege, getting men and guns for Zaragoza. And it was the people of the town, artisans, priests, women of the stamp of Agustina, even children, who fought at the barricades against Napoleon. When the French got a foothold in the town the fight became a carnage. And in the hour of confu- sion, Elizabeth Latimer recorded, "the doors of the lunatic asylum were burst open, and madmen, yelling and raging, mingled with the combatants." Was that the madhouse Goya painted?

The story of the siege of Zaragoza that the incomparable Richard Ford told is based on investigations made at the scene and not long after the war's end.

. . "The modern martyrs," Ford wrote, as Langdon-Davies has recalled,[1] "are those brave peasants who fought and died

---

[1]*Behind the Spanish Barricades.* By John Langdon-Davies. Robert M. McBride & Company. 1936.

like men; si monumentum quaeris, circumspice; look around
at the terrific ravages of the invader, which testify his relent-
less warfare, and the stubborn defence during the two sieges
which have rendered Zaragoza a ruin indeed, but immortal
in glory. One word of record. This city, like others in Spain,
rose after the executions of Murat on the Dos de Mayo,
1808; on the 25th Guillelmi, the governor, was deposed, and
the lower classes were organized by Tio Jorge Ibort, Gaffer
George, one of themselves; a nominal leader of rank being
wanted, one Jose Palafox, an Aragonese noble, was selected
because he was handsome, for in Spain, as in the East, personal
appearance is always influential. Palafox had served in the
Spanish royal bodyguard, and therefore, necessarily knew
nothing whatever of the military profession; but Tio Jorge
commanded, and with two peasants, Mariano Cerezo and
Tio Maria, for his right and left hand, did the fighting;
all the means of defense were 220 men, 100 dollars, 16 cannon and a few old muskets. Lefebure arrived June 15, 1808,
but paused and thus enabled Tio Jorge to prevent a coup-de-
main. To the French summons of surrender, the bold Tio
replied, 'War to the knife.' "

It is a retort, as we know, that has also been ascribed to
Palafox. But Ford, most rewarding of all guides to Spain,
holds in his admiration for Palafox. "Palafox," he observes,
"now went madder with vanity than any Gascon or Andaluz;
reposing under his laurels, he neglected every preparation for
future defense; meanwhile Buonaparte silently made ready
for his great revenge, and in three short months, while Juntas
were talking about invading France, crushed all the ill-
equipped armies of Spain at one blow. The city capitulated

February 20, 1809, the rest of Spain having looked on with apathy, while Infantado, with an idle army, did not even move one step to afford relief—*socorros de España tarde o nunca*. Lannes had pledged his honour that Palafox should depart free, and that no one should be molested; but he pillaged the temples, shed innocent blood, put Boggiera and others to death under prolonged torture; insulted Palafox and robbed him 'even of his shirt' and sent him to the dungeons of Vincennes. These two sieges cost the lives of nearly 60,000 brave men, which were lost for nothing, as the defence of the town was altogether a military mistake, and entirely the result of impulse and accident, the moving power of things in Spain. And now Tio Jorge is scarcely mentioned by name, for it would offend the pride of Spain's misleaders to admit the merit of a peasant, whose valour and intelligence shamed the cowardice and incapacity of the Alaches and Imazes. The Tio was a true son of the people of Spain, and his treatment from his so-called betters is purely Oriental and national."

Goya's equestrian portrait of Palafox is a commanding painting; in both art and life, however, it has its limitations. It is a gaudy masterpiece, a shouting of martial valor that by its stridency lessens its conviction. Resplendently uniformed and medalled Palafox swerves and rides valiantly, waving his shining sword at a city that burns red in the background. It seems fair to believe that Goya had in mind the liveliness of equestrian paintings by Titian or Velasquez in painting it; but he overreaches. The horse has been defended by Beruete unsuccessfully; even though he had no model at hand he could not have done worse. And the conception of Palafox seems a little more generous than it should be, as Richard Ford bears witness.

7

THE *Caprichos* were a prelude to perdition. The *Desastres* are a dance of death. In times of peace they seem stark and magnificent art. In time of war they are recalled again as the most brilliantly timeless pictures of war's dark backwash any man has ever drawn. Yet they are not all war scenes.

Goya etched what he had seen during the Napoleonic invasion intermittently from 1810—the date many of the etchings bear—to about 1820. In his house on the other side of the Manzanares from Madrid he worked with graver and plates, making a commentary sharper than the graver, more durable than the plates, more caustic than the acid that bit in the lines. He printed a few sets of the etchings, after his friend Cean Bermudez had arranged the series of 85 plates.

He meant to make a book of them. The title would be: "Fatal consequences of the sanguinary war with Bonaparte in Spain, with other emphatic *caprichos*, conceived, drawn and engraved by the original painter Don Francisco de Goya y Lucientes, in Madrid." That was the title Bermudez chose. The Academy's title, "Los Desastres de la Guerra," is far better.

They were to have appeared, Beruete suggests, in 1820. But by then the infamous Ferdinand VII was on the throne again. And there was in the plates a spirit of freedom and contempt for tyrants that was enough to account for the King's enmity toward Goya, material enough, indeed, to threaten him with garrotting. The very existence of the plates may—though this must be stated as inference, not proof—go a long way toward explaining the necessity for Goya's going into sanctuary at Duaso's house.

Sixty-five of the plates of the *Disasters of the War* are, as it has been pointed out, pictures of war and famine in Madrid. The ones on the famine run from the forty-eighth to the sixty-fifth. The rest are *caprichos enfaticos*, continuing the manner of the earlier *Caprichos* in a more furious and more somber mood.

The famine in Madrid lasted from September, 1811, to August, 1812, which dates their conception: they could not, for example, have been done in 1810. During that famine, Mesonero Romanos wrote, as Mayer recalls: "Men, women and children lay dying in the streets, they begged for a scrap of green stuff, for a potato, for a drop of soup however thin and bad. It was a scene of despair and pain. Terrible to see numberless human beings lying in the death-agony in the open street, by broad daylight to hear the lamentations of women, the crying of children, standing beside the bodies of their fathers and brothers. Twice a day parish carts removed corpses. The ceaseless groaning, the moaning of unfortunates in the pangs of death, terrified those who, hungry themselves, dared to go into the streets, and made them, too, like corpses. The air, full of poisonous vapors, seemed to spread a pall over the town. . . . I once counted several persons dead or dying in a walk of about three hundred paces, and ran home crying to throw myself into the arms of my mother, who was so terrified that for several months she would not let me go to school any more." What that child saw and remembered so well many years afterward when the perspective of time had cleared and history was a part of his recollections would be little compared to what Goya saw in Madrid.

Look at the plates of the *Desastres* if you would see what he saw. Here are some of the glories that Bonaparte brought to Madrid: Children starving in their own country while the soldiers of a dictatorial invader look on. Skeleton men starving while a better fed compatriot, a woman—perhaps an *afrancesada?*—passes them with bent head. Goya's caption is: "Lo peor es pedir"—"The worst is to have to beg." In another one, the gaunt Spaniard stands above a desperate heap of starving people. To the right, two cocked-hatted foreigners look on. And the title is: "Si son de otro linage"—"Do they belong to another race of men?"

Again, look at the woman bringing a cup to a group in the last stages of starvation. Lusterless, beyond caring, incidents of Napoleon's ambition, they wait for death. Under this one Goya says: "De que sirve una taza?"—"Of what use is a single cup?" How many moments more can they all live on that?

Their end is searingly suggested in the stark lines of the plate called "Las camas de la muerte"—"The beds of death" —where a single, hooded mourner walks despairingly past the shrouded rows of the dead. This is a plate that almost exists without detail, it is not a picture so much as it is the overwhelming spirit of a scene.

It was not that picture Elie Faure had in mind when he wrote: "Goya describes nothing and evokes everything, but his secret symbolism is nevertheless consistent, though perhaps involuntarily. It is a manner of seeing things, a manner of speaking and of being. Take, for example, the uniforms of the French soldiers in his etchings. They are not only badly proportioned, but shown as sketchily as possible; they have only a remote connection with the actual uniforms and might be those of any nation's army; he thus succeeds in conjuring up I know not what permanent army of sadists and executioners, and in this way enhances the terror and frightfulness of the drama. This is only one feature in the complexity of these sinister works, inspired by a sinister flame which is so ardent that it is impossible to translate its essence into words for those who have not examined them time after time. There are other features of the same kind, the summary landscape, for instance, made up of barely sketched indications, sometimes almost abstract—but for this reason endowing the eternal tragedy with a still more terrifying atmosphere, independent of time and almost independent of place. Black and white do the rest, with their very monotony, symbolizing unconsciously the alternatives of hope and despair to which mankind is for ever subjected."[1] But Elie Faure's words illuminate the plate as excellently as they do the others—and an important aspect of Goya's technique as well.

8

THERE is a striking modernity about these plates Goya drew a century and a quarter ago. The flung heaps of bodies waiting the anonymity of a common grave might be the victims of one of those contemporary air raids that our age has perfected as one contribution to progress. These dead are very like the dead that have filled the streets of Madrid again in our

[1]Francisco de Goya: *The Disasters of the War*. Oxford University Press.

time, and the streets of Guernica and Valencia and Barcelona when planes found their "military objectives" in the queues of women waiting with market baskets for the day's ration of food, or in streets full of children running around and playing so animatedly that they could easily be spotted from the sky.

Goya had seen these "fatal consequences of the sanguinary war with Bonaparte" in Madrid. He also saw, in the course of his journey to Zaragoza in the first year of the war, what brutal havoc the battles brought to the countryside. His pictures are not the dressed-up battle pieces that make, in the paintings of some celebrated artists, a kind of bright-colored masquerade of war.

On the contrary, he suggests, battle is not concerned so much with pleasing drama, unfortunately, as it is concerned with a kind of crude and impromptu surgery: to illustrate that he shows you how men seem when they are having bayonets run through them, how they look when they have lost an arm, a leg, or the head. He shows the slumped posture of blindfolded men tied to posts before the merciless, impersonal steel rifle barrels of the firing squads. He shows the dead being thrown into pits after all they own—to the last shred of clothing—has been stolen from them by the active corpse robbers, and the dying trampled under the boots of the conquerors.

For as Mayer has acutely observed: "Above all Goya introduces us to the realities of the 'small incidents' of war. The horrors which he depicts here are more dreadful than those of big battles. Side by side with well-known historic events, like the heroic deed of Agustina of Aragon, the massacre of

From the Disparates

THE NUN AND THE PHAN

the Marquess of Perales at Madrid, the burning of the Place Torquemada by Lasalle, the pillage of Cuenca by Caulaincourt's brigade, Goya shows the senselessness of warfare."

One of the *Desastres* shows Agustina of Aragon standing with a fuse beside the high wheels of the cannon she continued to fire when her lover was killed beside it. Goya knew her story, all Spain rang with it when he went up to Zaragoza in the first winter, as we saw. Byron wrote romantically of her in "Childe Harold" after he had been to Spain.

Goya's terse comments under the *Desastres* drive his points home with unexpected and sardonic remarks. "It will all be the same," as the dead are carried to the heaped dead. "So much and more," of another heap. And "The same thing in another place" of defenders fallen at the mouth of a cave.

"Por una navaja"—for carrying a pocket knife—the priest, crucifix in hand, has been garrotted by Napoleon's men. "Barbaros!"—the soldiers are shooting in the back the man tied to the tree. "A heroic deed!—With corpses!": Bodies hacked and stuck on a stumpy tree's branches.

"This I saw," he has written under a picture of a desperate woman, one child in her arms, another stumbling at her feet, trying to get them to safety, away from some violent attack. "And this also": The halting lines of women carrying infants away from the fighting, without hope. In "Madre infeliz!," a girl of three watches her dead young mother carried away.

9

IN MADRID, during those years, Goya could look at the spectacle of Joseph, once more secure behind the guns his brother sent, trying to govern for other peoples' good. Like all people who do good relentlessly, Joseph liked to be thanked. And the Spaniards did not thank him. Not for anything he did. When he began to clear the clutter of Madrid's jammed buildings by opening tree-planted parks here and there they only called him, for all his pains, "King Little-squares"— El Rey Plazuelo. When he devised a royal decoration to honor those that in his eyes had done bravely and well they noticed only the color of the ribbon that held his medal and called it the Order of the Eggplant. Goya took enormous care to make that color apparent in some portraits he did at the time. And their favorite names for him remained. When they were angry they called him scornfully the Intruder King—El Rey Intruso—with all its connotations of contempt for a man who reigns where he is not wanted. And when they were simply contemptuous they called him Pepe Botellas, Bottle Joe.

Joseph himself was not Napoleon's first choice. His first choice for the throne of Spain was Louis, King of Holland. But Louis refused the throne more definitely than Joseph was able to refuse. Napoleon's opinion of his elder brother Joseph was at times contemptuous, at best temperate. He was suspicious of him, too. In one of his letters to his young second wife Napoleon warned her against Joseph, who, he said, had learned loose ideas in Spain.

There was some ground for that. His wife, Julie, was not with him in Spain, and Sencourt remarks, after Grandmaison, that his mistresses were in turn "The Señora de Montehermoso, who spoke four languages, the Countess de Jaruco, and finally . . . Madame Nancy Derrieux."

Though the *chisperos*, the wits of Madrid, who found

endless material for sardonic laughter in everything that Pepe Botellas did, whether it was to rush prudently toward the border each time it seemed likely that his rule was about to end, or to profess a vast interest in bullfighting by way of currying popular favor, insisted that their intruder king preferred wine to women. They supplied the song:

> *No quiere Pepe*
> *Ninguna bella.*
> *Quiere acostarse . . .*
> *Con la botella.*

10

In the Autumn of 1810 Goya was chosen, with Maella and Napoli, to select fifty paintings from Spain that were to be sent to Napoleon, a man who never failed to try to cart off what was valued most in the countries whose people he assured he had invaded for their own best interests.

The intention, obviously, was to have Goya pick the best works of Spain's best artists. But—as Beruete has pointed out —the paintings, listed by Viñaza, that the three men got together were by no means the best Spain could show. The most lamentable "masters of the rear ranks" were included and praised to the skies with an irony that would escape Joseph. And when it became necessary to put in something by recognized masters—Ribera, Zurbarán, Murillo, Velasquez, Cano—the French were offered minor works, or replicas. Though, as it turned out, they never got any of them.

Joseph had no illusions about his rôle in Spain. Sencourt makes that clear. He points out that by the time Joseph had got to Vitoria he wrote Napoleon that the enterprise would be a failure. At Burgos he wrote that opinion again. And his busy letter-writing reached a climax on the subject on the 24th of July, 1808, when he was the first to give Napoleon the idea that Napoleon later on adopted as his own: "Your glory will be destroyed in Spain." He had discovered soon after he reached Madrid that the whole nation was in arms against Napoleon. The Constitution that Napoleon had drawn up for Spain was better than what the people had under Carlos or would get under Ferdinand. But they didn't want it. What they wanted was to throw the invaders out of Spain.

At the bayonet point, the foreign army could for a time seem to dominate Spain. Yet at Bailen the Spaniards showed they could defeat Napoleon's men. Armed with sticks and knives and old muskets they did not look like an army capable of facing Napoleon. But they were willing to go on and on. They could not be beaten. They would not be beaten.

Joseph had the wit to see that. He ruled at the point of Napoleon's bayonets only. The first autumn of Joseph's rule he had to leave Madrid. Bailen had shown the Spaniards they were capable of having Spain to themselves. The *guerrilleros* were heroic. The Spaniards had made Napoleon's troops run for it. And when they surrendered at Bailen, Joseph cleared out. Madrid belonged to the Spaniards again—for a time. Then Napoleon came back and got Joseph back on the throne —for a time.

It was while Joseph was out and before Napoleon came to lift him back that Goya was referred to as painter to the King of Spain, which is one proof that he was not an *afrancesado*.

The glories Napoleon promised the Spaniards if they would

submit to his noble rule were not very appealing. It may have been piety that made the Spaniards not delighted with Napoleon's promise that he would abolish the Inquisition. He himself had just been excommunicated. Or it may have been an idea that they preferred to manage their own affairs in religion as in everything else.

Goya painted various portraits of the Frenchmen who came to Madrid with Joseph, but the belief that he was a painter to Joseph himself seems thoroughly doubtful. Beruete has pointed out that though he received a nomination for Joseph's decoration, the Royal Order of Spain (popularly known, as we have already noted, as the Order of the Eggplant), he never used it. Furthermore, he was listed simply as *pintor*, a painter, while Maella was listed as First Court Painter. And when the armies of Spain and Wellington were in Madrid, Goya was called painter to the king—which would scarcely mean the king that army was there to drive out.

The story of Goya's portrait of Joseph is an astonishing tale. It begins with an eminent Peruvian called Don Tadeo Bravo de Rivera, who happened to be in Madrid at the time. Goya had painted Bravo before the war began. After the war began Bravo took a good deal of interest in affairs. So in 1809, when the town officials of Madrid decided they wanted a picture to show their good will toward Joseph, they asked Tadeo Bravo to choose the painter, the best painter he could find.

And he chose Goya. Why the town counselors had to get Don Tadeo to discover Goya for them, is not clear. Beruete, who has brilliantly pieced the whole story together from the researches of Feriz and Foxa, does not explain that. At any rate, Bravo said the painting would cost not less than 15,000 reales, in a letter dated February 27, 1810. He also delicately mentioned that he had advanced part of the price to Goya. Which suggests that Goya had not been prosperous during the French occupation—though he could have been, by becoming an *afrancesado*.

The painting Goya produced is a fearful and wonderful creation. I saw it, in its last phase, in the Madrid town hall, just outside the office of the fattest mayor in Europe. It is an allegory. And what an allegory. A robust woman in bare feet and tablecloth robes represents Madrid. She wears a coronet: Madrid is la coronada villa. She leans on the shield of Madrid, the familiar picture of the bear pawing at a tree. She is pointing, however, to a medallion, which is held by winged angels. Above them, another angel leans back to blow a resounding blast on a long trumpet. At the foot of the wide goddess of Madrid a lop-eared dog sits placidly, taking no interest whatever in what is going on.

The medallion is the whole point of the picture. It was meant to hold a portrait of Joseph, made from a print that Bravo lent Goya. And for a time, Joseph's face was there. But not for long. When Joseph went, his face was painted out. When he returned, it was painted back. When he went for the last time, his face disappeared for good. But that was not the end of change in that picture.

It was changed so much, that shield, that merely by looking at it, in those years of tumult, one could tell the state of affairs in Spain. In 1812, when the armies of Spain and Wellington advanced on Madrid, Joseph had to leave town. And the picture had to be changed. It had to be changed quickly.

Joseph's face was painted out. In place of Joseph's monarchic face the word *Constitution* was painted in. But the reign of Joseph was not over. He came back to Madrid, shielded by Napoleon's bayonets. So the portrait of Joseph, that had in August been painted out, was in December put back in place of the word.

But Joseph's reign did not last long, this time. By spring he had been forced to leave Madrid forever. Ferdinand was on his way back. Thereupon, Joseph was painted out for the second time, and for the second time the word *Constitution* appeared on the angel-guarded shield, painted there by Dionisio Gomez, a pupil of Goya, since Goya could no longer be troubled.

Ferdinand was stung to fury every time he saw the word *Constitution*. He had sworn to uphold it, of course, but he was really determined to smash it. Therefore, he ordered the shield painted over again. In place of the word, the face of Ferdinand, painted by some anonymous hack, appeared. The painting was so badly done that in 1826 the authorities paid Lopez 2000 reales to paint another portrait of Ferdinand there.

And even that was not the end of the matter. Some time in the early eighteen forties, when Ferdinand had gone the way of all dictators, his face in its turn was swept from the shield, and the book of the Constitution took its place.

Finally, in 1872, Ferriz and Foxa suggested to the mayor of Madrid that if all the layers of changing faces and notations were removed, Goya's painting might be revealed. Palmaroli set to work, and went down through the stratifications. But when he got to the bottom there was not much

Goya to be found. Other scrapers had been before him. The space had to be filled again. What should they put there this time? *Constitution* again?

"No!" said Foxa. "By no means! In Spain reaction is always waiting for us and continually reappears; this word has been erased from the picture several times, and we have now to give the picture a lasting character." It was then, according to Beruete, that they decided to write on the shield the words it bears now, words forever associated with Goya's Madrid: *Dos de Mayo*.

II

GOYA took a sword to the Duke of Wellington with the idea of carving out his bowels. Goya turned from the easel and wrenched a pistol out of a drawer to shoot the Duke through his right eye. Goya very nearly smashed a vase over Wellington's head. All because, when Goya was painting the Duke's portrait the Duke made some remark that Goya did not like.

It's a beguiling legend, and it does a certain romantic honor to both those violent and distinguished men. Even Beruete says he has heard the painter "seized hold of some pistols which he had on the table," before finding the episode improbable. The others, of course, seldom qualify the fable at all.

Anyway, it's the least important part of the story. We have three paintings of Wellington by Goya, and that extraordinary drawing now in the British Museum which I am inclined to think was the original sketch for all the paintings. Wellington's latest biographer, Guedalla, in his chapter on the Duke's Peninsular campaign, says—writing of the occasion when the drawing was made:

"Indeed, the victory might have been still more crushing if a Spanish force, which he had posted at a ford behind the French, had been capable of simple obedience. But Carlos de España had decamped from Alba de Tormes, and the French slipped by. Spain was at Alba, though—the sinister, uncomprehended Spain of macabre *Caprichos* and sardonic portraits of egregious Bourbons and preposterous grandees— watching through the sharp eyes of Francisco Goya y Lucientes. For Goya watched him, as he rode in that night from Salamanca, if the note appended to his sketch can be believed; and the strange drawing, with its unavoidable suggestion of an ascetic interrupted in his cell or a drowning man restored unexpectedly to the surface, records the exhausted victor— unshaven, hollow-eyed, the damp hair plastered to his forehead, a little shaken by the spent bullet which had bruised his thigh—a wild-eyed, unfamiliar Wellington, as Goya saw him on that summer night in a Spanish village."

This is the text of the note—some one in Goya's family wrote it, so that would probably be his son or the grandson who was in Bordeaux with him (and who became a grandee) —as Guedalla copied it:

Un dibujo hecho en Alba de Tormes despues de la Batalla de Arapiles de Duque de Wellington por hel que se hizo el retrato.

"It appears to follow," Guedalla writes, without filling in the intervening steps, "that Goya's three oil paintings of Wellington (equestrian portrait painted for W., now at Stratfield Saye; portrait with hat, formerly in the possession of Alava now in U. S. A.; portrait without hat in the possession of Duke of Leeds, now in the National Portrait Gallery) were founded on the British Museum drawing. If this view is accepted, the agreeable anecdotes of Goya's violent onslaughts on W. during a sitting at Madrid must be dismissed."

Yet not dismissed too cavalierly. They are truer than truth because they dramatize the quality of furious independence in Goya.

12

AT Cadiz the Cortes met. There is every reason on earth to criticize it. There is its immortality as justification. It was weak and wandering and absurd. And it was indomitable. They had been driven down there by slow and bloody stages. A gathering to make possible a rule by law was at the mercy of rule by slaughter. One may read innumerable pages showing the weakness of the gathering, their shortcomings in going about their work. What one may marvel at is their ever going about their work at all.

Month after month they worked at making a Constitution for Spain. They had at the same time other things to do. They were the only Spanish power of any influence in Spain. Their kings had deserted them. They had a war to carry on against the troops of the most powerful man in the world. When, in 1812, they finally created a Constitution it was a document that had the magnificence of belief in the rights of man.

The Constitution of Cadiz may seem a rather conservative document in modern eyes. In it, as Hume has noted, "the abstract sovereignty of the nation was reasserted, the Catholic religion alone acknowledged, and the monarchy was to be hereditary under the parliamentary constitution. The legislative power was vested in the single chamber Cortes with the

King, the executive in the King's ministers only, and the judicial in the judges; the Parliaments were to be indirectly elected by equal electoral districts of 70,000 souls, on a residential manhood suffrage, and were to be summoned yearly, the royal veto upon acts being confined to three rejections, after which the acts became law in despite of the King's veto. The monarch was prohibited from absenting himself from the realm, or marrying without the permission of the Cortes, and the succession was fixed on the old Spanish basis, like that of England, but the Infante Don Francisco de Paula, the reputed child of Godoy, was excluded, as was also the Queen of Etruria." This was a large step toward creating a republic in Spain. But it left Church and King secure.

In the blackest time of that foreign invasion when the regular army of Spain had gone over to the enemy or scattered, when the *juntas* could not rule and the various Spanish commands were scattered by wedges the troops of Napoleon had driven between the regions, it was the indomitable *guerrilleros* who kept alive the spirit of Spanish freedom.

One of the bravest of these was Juan Martín, called El Empecinado, whose band swooped down again and again to strike at the foreign troops in Castile. Their equipment was obsolete, their organization was grotesque, their uniforms were the ragged peasant costumes of the race. But they could fight, and they knew the plains and the mountains of their native Castile with a thoroughness the soldiers of Napoleon could never equal.

Goya painted the portrait of El Empecinado. He wears the uniform tunic he must have worn when he rode beside Wellington into Madrid.

Goya's painting shows him, stalwart and unconquerable, the dark face and the arrogant force, a warrior who fought for a renegade king who had him tortured when he returned. When Juan Martín was being led to the gallows one of the king's officers jeered at him. He showed Juan Martín the sword that had been taken away from him. Juan Martín knocked down his guards, got to the officer who held his sword, wrenched it from him and killed him with it.

English historians of the Peninsular War are apt to regard askance the *guerrilleros* who were fighting for their lives, people and homes. Wellington (who had said of his own wharf-rat replacements: "By God. I don't know what the enemy will think of these men, but they fill me with terror") deplored them. Elizabeth Latimer quotes Sir William Napier's *History of the Peninsular War:* "The guerilla system in Spain was the offspring of disorder. . . . It is in such a warfare that habits of unbridled license, of unprincipled violence, and disrespect for the rights of property are quickly contracted, and render men unfit for the duties of citizens." Whose property was Spain?

Hume said: "The greatest of the guerilla chiefs who had fought the French was the chivalrous Empecinado—a mere peasant named Juan Martín, but a born commander of men. On Fernando's return from France the Empecinado's immense services to the country had been rewarded by close imprisonment, until the revolt of Riego set him free. When the Constitution fell the Empecinado escaped to Portugal, but was captured near the frontier at the same time as Fernando entered Madrid (November, 1823). He was," Hume remarks revealingly, "kept by the local authorities at Roa for the next ten months, suffering the most revolting tortures in prison, being brought out every market day in an iron cage to be exposed to the insults of the crowd." What kind of a crowd was that? "For four days at a time he was kept without food or drink, confined in one position; and his prayers that he should promptly be put out of his misery only brought upon him fresh persecution. In vain the English ambassador protested to the king against such inhumanity; the Empecinado refused to acknowledge any crime or beg for mercy, as he had formerly refused the bribe of a peerage to desert the Constitution, and he was at length condemned to the gallows."

It was on St. Patrick's Day, 1813, that Joseph finally left Madrid forever. He overloaded himself with plunder. "Heaping together from the robbery of churches and monasteries what treasure he could," as Sencourt observes, and "taking what treasures he could from the Prado, Raphaels, Titians, Velasquezes and Corregios," Joseph prepared for his last flight from Spain.

Disaster overtook him at Vitoria. The Spaniards and the English threatened to cut off his escape to France. Joseph was in a panic. He abandoned everything—the paintings, the money, the wine, the jewels and the crown. Perhaps he would miss the crown least.

VIII
The Dream of Reason
[1814–1824]

VIII

The Dream of Reason

[1814–1824]

I

Goya's last decade in Spain began in the spring of 1814, when Ferdinand the Unbeloved was restored to the throne, and an indication of the character of those years was given at once. The dream of reason produced a monster again.

The Spaniards who had thought Ferdinand would be grateful to a people who had fought and starved for him in the years of his absence were disenchanted soon after he returned to Spain. He not only broke his word to support the Constitution of Cadiz but announced that any man who spoke in favor of it would be put to death. In the night a few days before his return to Madrid he sent soldiers to jail the members of the Cortes, and Hume records that poets, men-of-letters, journalists, nobles, lawyers, officers, actors and every other person known to have liberal ideas were also taken to dungeons.

As he had used cutthroats and assassins in Aranjuez six years before to terrorize his father—by now in Rome—into abdicating, so now he used them to terrorize Madrid. For now, as Hume observes, "the country at large was a prey to a reactionary fever of the worst kind; Fernando thenceforward was influenced alone by the base *camarilla* which had led him from humiliation to humiliation before the triumphal car of Napoleon. He had abandoned the country to itself, and had not raised a finger in those six terrible years of its death struggle with the foreign invader. His had been the name upon the lips of thousands who had gone to their death cheerfully that he might reign in the land of his fathers. The country in a frenzy of loyalty brought him back to the throne for which he had done nothing; and the returns he gave were chains, exile, and death to those who had fought hardest, and struggled most, to shake off the yoke of the foreigner." This was El Deseado.

The throne of Spain became the scorn of Europe. It was known that Ferdinand's *camarilla* included some of the most contemptible blackguards on the Continent. The Spanish colonies in America benefited somewhat; they found it easier to win their battles for independence, and the United States got Florida. Revolts broke out all over Spain, as well. They were put down with inconceivable ferocity, but the plotting went on in secret. The nation was bankrupt. Ferdinand restored the Inquisition and announced a censorship that included the works of Gibbon and Voltaire in its proscription.

Goya, living in the Quinta del Sordo, had material enough to draw on for pictures of a world in nightmare.

The hope of freedom rose again when Riego led the successful insurrection against the king that brought about three years of rule under the Constitution. Once more the Inquisition was abolished, and once more Ferdinand swore to keep his promises. The crowds sang "Trágala, perro!"—Swallow it, dog!—to those who had scorned the Constitution. But the European powers sent troops under Angoulême to support

Ferdinand, and again Ferdinand revoked his promises. Riego, the hero of the rebellion, was decked in a green liberty cap, drawn through the streets behind a donkey, and hanged.

It was now Goya painted the *Dos de Mayo* and its sequel, as well as the portrait of Palafox; obviously they could not be done while Joseph was on the throne of Spain.

The story that when Ferdinand returned he said to Goya, "You deserve to be garrotted, but because you are a great artist we have decided to pardon you," would be better if it supplied the salt of a Goyesque reply.

It was the next year he painted the best of the portraits of himself, the head aslant as though he leaned from the easel to look in a mirror that showed him a face intent and unsmiling, carrying buoyantly the mastery of nearly seventy years.

And when he wanted to do so, he painted portraits of others, the Duque de San Carlos, aloof and hidalgoesque, proud, apparently, of having been Ferdinand's majordomo at Valençay as well as the lover of Madame Talleyrand, the Duchess of Abrantes looking at a sheet of music for all the world as though she would recall the world of the eighteenth century, the young Duke of Osuna, who had been even younger in the days of the picnics and the fêtes galantes when the Duchess of Alba was his mother's rival.

In 1817 Goya went to Seville and painted the engagingly worldly picture of SS. Justa and Rufina with the amiable lion at their feet, a painting that was always said to disturb the meditations of the priest officiating in sight of it in the great Cathedral.

[209]

IT WAS in 1815 that Goya's undying interest in the bullring was shown again in the superb series of etchings on bullfighting, the *Tauromaquia*.

Goya went far back in time for that record, showing the way the Spaniards of old fought bulls in open fields, on horseback and afoot, proceeding to the legendary Gazul, who is supposed to have begun to formalize the sport in the eleventh century, then showing the Moors waving their burnooses in the manner of the latter-day *capas*, the early use of dartlike *banderillas*, and a nobleman's kill.

Goya's overdressed etching of Charles V—the emperor in a more powerful line than Charles IV—as a bullfighter suggests that he might just have finished sitting for Titian before entering the plaza at Valladolid. The fabulous Cid fights a bull with a lance, alone, and in the next plate a crowd of people attack a bull with lances.

Martincho was a favorite subject of Goya. Here he is placing banderillas, and there he shows more intrepidity than grace by sitting on a chair, his feet manacled in irons, facing a bull in the plaza at Zaragoza. Pepe-Hillo and Pedro Romero appear in action. Ceballos outdoes them all by riding astride one bull in pursuit of another. Bulls die, horses die, dogs set to attack the bulls die, bullfighters die—and even a spectator meets death when the Mayor of Torrejon is killed in the ring at Madrid.

Several of the etchings are dated 1815. Yet few of the proofs he made in the Quinta del Sordo were sold in his time. They were not widely sold until after the death of his son.

Goya's title was: "Thirty-three prints that represent different suertes and acts of the art of bullfighting, conceived and engraved in etchings in Madrid by Don Francisco de Goya y Lucientes."

In his old age, at Bordeaux, when he had taken up the new art of lithography, he returned again to the bullring. He did these in 1825 when he was nearly eighty years old, and he may have used a magnifying glass. Gaulón, whose portrait he also did, printed them. They are: "El famoso Americano Mariano Ceballos," the picador tossed by a bull, the divided arena, and the *Diversión de España*—the sport of Spain. They deserve Rothenstein's praise when he says of them that "These are executed in the most superb style, with a vigor of conception and execution which Goya himself never equalled in his previous work—the whole science of modern composition is to be found in these four drawings—and which have never been equalled since. An artist's early work may generally be said to be his most serious rival, but in the Taureaux de Bordeaux Goya, at the age of eighty odd years [*sic*] actually surpassed himself. Movement takes the place of form—the tremulous excitement of the crowds of spectators watching the sweaty drama in the ring, the rush to and fro of the *toreros*, the stubborn strength of the short powerful goaded brute with the man impaled on his horns, the dust and glitter and riot of the scene is rendered in a most extraordinary manner. Three succeeding generations of artists have helped themselves with both hands from these prints, but left them not a farthing the poorer."

He lived in these years mainly in the house he had bought years before near the Puente de Segovia. It was called—in a wit as unsparing and as commonplace as Spain knows— as the Quinta del Sordo: the Deaf Man's Villa.

The royal hunting preserves were nearby, and there Goya went hunting when he wanted to, whether his official position was enough to make the keepers believe he had a right there or not.

And he had quite a lot of land of his own; nearly 65 acres, with a two-story house and a view across the Manzanares— that inadequate stream so many witticisms are floated on: Cervantes called it a rivulet with the reputation of a river. It might remind you of his painting for the Osunas of the view from that side; the palace rising enormous and oyster white and the round dome of San Francisco el Grande containing the painting of San Isidro he had set so much store by thirty years and more ago.

For company he had at first, perhaps, Josefa, the faithful Josefa, who died as inconspicuously as she had lived, some time after the will they made together in 1811 was signed. Then came Leocadia Weiss, a preposterous woman Mayer says was a cousin once removed; perhaps not soon enough. She is supposed to have married one Isidro Weiss, whose father was a Bavarian emigré, and Isidro deserted her. Rosario, her daughter, whose efforts in art we have discussed, was also, no doubt, in the Quinta.

The paintings on the walls of the rooms in the Quinta del Sordo were done for no man's pleasure but his own. They form a personal testament. As autobiography they have a considerable interest, as art they seem to me Goya's profoundest and most magnificent work. Here, after all the years of putting his deepest opinions of the world around him into his plates for the etchings, he painted for his own satisfaction an incomparable series of *Caprichos* in color.

Las pinturas negras de Goya, they are called in Spain. The black paintings. The color is sombre. But there is flame in the shadows, and a demonic gayety lights the faces of those characters in the gallery of the damned. They trouble midnight and the noon's repose. In their swift broken lights and shadows of impressionism they were to influence a generation of French painters who are today's old masters of modernity.

But when he cleared the long room on the first floor of its Spanish chests and furniture and stood on planks to put the color on those walls it was less the mood to experiment that stirred him than the mood of indignation. *Saturn Devouring His Children*, and the two men, sinking to their knees in quicksand yet using their last moments to smash each other's heads open, are scathing comments on war between brothers in Spain.

The child, Rosario, may have come into the room and found the walls interestingly wet to the touch and glowing with strange pictures before she was hurried out to play in the garden by a Leocadia already indignant at what she saw. But Goya worked on, painting on the first floor's walls the sad *Manola* and the *Two Old Friars*, the *Fete of San Isidro*, the *Witches' Sabbath*, *Judith with the Head of Holofernes*, and the devouring *Saturn*. And before he was done there were eight more in the room upstairs that looked out over the sloping country toward the Manzanares, the high range of the Guadarramas, and Madrid.

4

ON one wall he painted a girl. She stands there, lonely and lost, as though haunted by some vision of the past in the murals before her. There is a memory of beauty in her face, yet her posture against the balustraded rock is lusterless, and her veiled eyes look beyond the room. The mantilla and the dark dress and the silver slippers relate her to the dancers of the tapestry cartoons and the *majas* on the balcony, but she has neither the gayety of those women nor their air of certainty of living in a world that could never change.

A world has changed around her, an era has gone down to ruin in blood and cannonading, she has only an unreturning past to remember. Her breasts are white through the lace, and she is a little *loca*. Is she the faithful Pepa, forever replenishing the earth and almost always in vain? Is she the *amarga* Leocadia? Or is she one more memory of a Duchess who had neither age nor years of tumult nor change to face, as she would look, in Goya's imagination, if she returned to be the *maja* of the time of havoc?

There was a narrow panel to decorate and on that wall he painted two old men expressing his idea of age and its burden and the greater burden of deafness. In the foreground he painted an ancient, white-bearded and a little bent over a long crooked stick that makes a streak of light. He has an air of wise and weary resignation. The other one is all vacuous energy. He has a thin face and a sharp nose. And he is bellowing in the ear of the old man with a blatant excessiveness

that only a deaf man could record. It seems to me unquestion-
able that Goya meant it so. The old man, furthermore, has a
drooping left eyelid that we recognize in the Lopez portrait
of Goya.

Saturn Devouring His Children is the most astounding and
the most famous of the Quinta murals. It is an inescapable
speculation to wonder what guests at Goya's table thought
when they looked up to see that on the dining-room wall.
Saturn is a lean and half-crouching madman. His body comes
out of the shadows. Blood lies in a broad sash over the shoulders of the headless torso he holds, and it has flowed down
and reddened the tops of the clenching hands. Saturn's face
is brown, his eyeballs are white-rimmed and staring, brown
streaks his face and greenish gray hair. The inspiration came
from Rubens's painting, without question. The symbolism is
for Madrid and Spain to understand best. One may say with
Aguilera[1] that it suggests the rancor in the royal family, the
fury of the war. In any event it is a superbly painted picture,
and perhaps the most disturbing mural for a dining room this
world has known.

In another part of the room he painted Judith and the
Head of Holofernes. Judith is a full-breasted girl in shadows.
She looks to the right and downward. Under the knife held
high in her right hand there is the shadowy silhouette of
a turbaned, Dante-nosed head bowed under the knife, the
hands raised in prayer. He painted rose-colors on Judith's
cheeks and arms. The rest is gray-green, silver and black, the
body of Judith in her loose dress lit by a greenish light. The
upthrust arm that holds the knife is brighter than the knife,

[1]*Las Pinturas Negras de Goya.* Emiliano M. Aguilera. Madrid. 1936.

[215]

and so it carries the eye to the blade in the shadow. Holofernes is still asleep. Judith's servant is praying. Aguilera has pointed out that in this painting Goya made a symbolical allusion to the Spanish women who fought with enormous valor against the French during Spain's war of independence. Just as Judith fought for Bethulia.

A dog's head, ghostly and appealing, rises suppliant from the cloudy void of eternity in another panel Goya painted for the room. The dog is gazing intently at something only he sees in the yellow obscurity at the right. One used to return over and over again to that panel in the Prado, and wonder what it is the dog sees. It may be the shadow of a dead master. It may be the head of another dog, or the god of all dogs. There is nothing uncompleted about the painting. The form proves that—though some eminent commentators, misled, I think, by the simplicity of the conception, have suggested that it is unfinished. It is a composed, complete picture as it stands, and any one who has ever owned a dog will find it haunting.

I have been unable to find anything to confirm a natural supposition that in putting the portrait of the dog there in that room with the other murals painted for his pleasure alone, Goya drew a dog he had owned and liked and lost. A mild theory like that is probably enough for one picture in a room where most of the other paintings offer fields for speculation singularly vast.

It may be a dog Goya still had in the Quinta. The composition may have been suggested by the dog's habit of sitting against the yellow light of a window, and looking up at Goya as he painted. Certainly dogs are not rare in his pic-

FROM THE WALLS OF THE QUINTA DEL SORDO

tures. Fierce mongrels barking at the night, sleek hunting dogs, the king's collared retrievers and the small yapping pets of the duchesses and the marquesas, strays and thoroughbreds and gentlemen rankers of their own lost legion, they are a part of Goya's art. Lincoln might have said: he must have liked dogs, he painted so many of them.

There is the cold and forlorn relative of all Dalmatians who stands in the snowy foreground of the tapestry cartoon for winter at one end of the scale, and the arrogant poodle who barks defiantly at his mistress' feet in the Liria Palace portrait of the Duchess of Alba at the other. A muff of a dog lies beside the toy carriage in the portrait of the Osunas. The Marquesa de Pontejos has her ribboned pug. Fat Charles IV has his fat hunting dog: the two of them must have followed game in a stately, liverish way.

The dog in the scene in the witches' kitchen belongs to demonology, but, on the other hand, the lion gently licking the toes of Santa Rufina is only a Newfoundlander in masquerade. I think the dogs at the foot of the fop-haunted *maja* in the *Capricho* called "Who is the more infatuated?" are significantly of the breed of the disagreeable dog in the rare *Capricho* of the man patting a dog he hates before women who hate him. The ribbed apparition in the Quixote drawing is half borzoi and half cur, the bull-baiting mastiffs of the bullfight lithograph have more courage than their masters. A sad setter lies on the ground before the kite fliers; and the Spanish mastiffs appear again in the painting on tin of the bull-baiting that shows Seville's Torre de Oro in the background. Goya, never at ease in painting horses, inclined to give even the most domestic cats—as in the portrait of young Manuel Osorio—a hair-raising balefulness, proficient in painting birds, was most thoroughly at home in painting dogs. There are some fine portraits of them in his gallery.

5

THE revellers of the San Isidro pilgrimage are a wild and disenchanted band as Goya painted them in one of the great murals of the Quinta. Long ago he had painted the same scene for the Osunas, but that was in another age and in a younger mood, a country festival below the walls of Madrid, in light spirits and light colors. Now he repeated the subject savagely, and with enormous force. On a dark road below black rolling hills a procession marches back to Madrid. In the foreground there is a mound of faces bawling some tune played by a madman with a guitar. Stumbling, drunken, lost, they keep on their way by habit, not by intelligence, people with beaked faces, men cloaked and women in mantillas disarrayed. The picture is a magnificent triumph of composition. It may all be a parable on the return of Ferdinand, or of the march of Napoleon, whose round Italian eyes and forelock seem to come out of one face in the procession.

A great black spiral-horned goat wearing a cassock preaches to a crowd of women. On that long wall Goya painted his forceful opinion of superstition and sorcery. Far to the right a seated figure stands out. She is alone, a little aloof, as far away as she can get from the cassocked leader of the black mass. She is the most composed of the women there. The others—from the hag bent over bead-counting fingers behind the black goat to the end of the mound—are desperately intent on what he is saying. They all have mouths agape, eyes dilated with avid interest, the looks Goya gave them to show their credulity, the madness of the possessed. She is a little apart. But she is there, one with the others in spite of herself, clutching at her little muff, and listening. She suggests a wraith of the Duchess of Alba, but more, she symbolizes those who were not quite strong enough to keep apart from the fascination of the rites of sorcery.

Over another door he painted another broad-stroked fling at the ignominy of growing old. Two human antiquities are eating soup. The woman, at the left, has skull-tight brown skin and the shrivelled grin of a crone. The man, on the right, is little more than shoulders behind a skeleton's head. She clutches a silver spoon in brown bony hands above a bowl. He seems to be reading something to her that makes her turn her head in grim satisfaction as they eat.

Two girls laughing at a man in some trouble dire and undivulged fill another panel. Goya painted them so the light strikes the three faces in a splash of whitish yellow. The girls have dark shadows for eyes, their cheeks curve in smiles that are directed at the man while the man thinks only of himself, apparently beyond caring. It is one of Goya's great paintings, a somber triumph of sardonic sensibility. To reproduce it is usually futile, the tones are too dark for white paper. You can only remember looking at it and thinking God help any man who is laughed at that way by two pretty girls. You do not feel that it is for anything spiritual they are laughing at him, or that his agonized abstraction indicates that he is unaware of the reason for their laughter.

In the same sardonic mood he painted on a tall panel a scene of five men bending over a paper that one of them, seated, is reading aloud. They huddle conspiratorially. What do they read? The dark-bearded, greenish-white central figure expresses the greatest intelligence, the full thrust of the scene is in him, the others are a border of listeners, figures in a *Capricho*, absorbed in some edict, some news of catastrophe or victory, that must be guardedly discussed.

In the painting called *Visión Fantástica* the scene shows a high plain with a battle in the foreground, troops and irregulars deploying, while two fantastic figures of heroic size, sailing through the air, point to a sheer cliff with a castle on it. This wall Goya painted in brighter colors and in far more detail than most of the others. The sky is filled with stormy sunlight, the rose-red cloak of one of the figures is striking, light lies in pools on the shelf of the rock where riders advance. Is it only a vision? Or is it an impression of the siege of San Sebastian during the Napoleonic war? Or do those figures, as some believe, tell the people on the ground that their cause should not be to kill one another but to attack together the rulers of the castle?

Seated on nothing, their legs intertwined, four inscrutable figures sail over a yellow and white river and a haunted landscape in the painting called *Las Parcas*. They are well-fed figures of evil. If it were not for the fourth you might call them The Fates and be done with their identities. That fourth, sitting upright, his arms bound behind him, may be their prisoner. He may be a man Goya knew, and this a sardonic picture of his predicament. The Fate of the scissors is there. But who are the other two? One carries a figurine of a child, the other looks through a glass. They may only be four witches out for the night's sail.

The other sardonic vision of the San Isidro pilgrims carried his opinions of the times further. Here the procession is led by a symbolic group: one is a Spanish grandee wearing the order of the Golden Fleece. He is of the past; his cap and his vandyke suggest the imperial age of the Philips. On his right is a fat and angry-looking nun. Behind them, more nuns, and then the procession wanders towards the horizon. It has been supposed, and with considerable reason, that in this Goya unmistakably alluded to the forces Ferdinand brought back to Spain with him. One may accept that. But here, as in the others, it is the sombre magnificence of the paintings that strikes you long before you look for the ideas. Yet it is the ideas that give them their force and passion. Paintings as strong as these are not based on the simple desire to give color to a wall.

On a long panel, two men are sinking in quicksand. They are antagonists, armed with clubs. Blood streams down the face of the man at the left. He is nearly spent but he is still fighting; the man facing him is merciless. At the right, against looming mountains, the bulk of a monster lies dead. What is the monster they—or one of them—killed? Why are they spending their last moments clubbing one another to death instead of trying to help themselves out of the quicksand and back to peaceful life? This is one of the simplest and most vigorously painted of all the scenes from the Quinta del Sordo. It is a parable of Spain, of the barbarism of civil war, that is timeless.

6

He worked also, during these years in the Quinta del Sordo between 1814 and 1819, on a new series of etchings. These he called *Disparates*. They are somewhat like the *Caprichos*, or some of the *Desastres de la Guerra*. And even more so than the *Caprichos* they elude the explanation of literal obviousness. Instead, they have the sardonic swing and bite of the murals he was putting on the walls of his house at the same time. They have sometimes been called the *Sueños*, or the *Proverbios*.

Goya seldom capitalized on his later series of prints. It may be that he was indifferent. It may be that he only did them for his own pleasure, to express in art his judgment of the world he lived in. Furthermore, with Ferdinand and the Inquisitors watching for every sign of heresy and scorn of the crown, it was futile to try to sell them publicly. As the foremost artist in Spain, and as the king's painter at least in title, he had anyway more freedom than many other men. But it had been shown that no man, no matter what his degree, could go against Ferdinand's wishes. Goya took that risk. In spite of the peril, he went ahead and made his points. They may seem allegorical. But no one looking at them could by any stretch of hypocritical interpretation claim that they were resonant endorsements of Ferdinand.

One of his most unforgettable *Disparates* shows a group of people huddled on a rotten branch. What need is there of an explanation to that? Every man can see in it something sharp and compelling. One may choose to interpret it as signifying the way the old and unfortunate are left uncared for. Or one may say that in it Goya meant to symbolize the useless and decayed life of the nobility. It may, for that matter, symbolize the decadence of Spain. But in any case it is an incomparable etching, drawn with a magnificent use of

THE DEAD BRANCH — DISPARATE RIDICULO

Goya fecit año 1819

San Anton, Madrid

CHRIST IN THE GARI

light and shade, a bite and penetration in these shadowed faces, a hopelessness of posture that haunts the mind.

He commented again on matrimony, showing man and woman bound together unwillingly. He showed a woman riding a white horse over a multitude of people—which may represent a woman of valor who has outraged convention.

In another, he showed an elephant being coaxed by men bearing tablets. This may represent the people faced by wily priests of various faiths. It has been pointed out that the elephant is gelded and without tusks. And the men of faith are dressed in the Moorish as well as other costumes.[1]

The *Disparate* of the men flying with great bats' wings expressed graphically the idea that what a bird can do man can learn to do. It is, of course, an idea that was old to the Greeks, and that may have been best expressed by the artists of the Renaissance. Goya drew men with their arms grasping the upper edges of the looped wings, their feet helping to control the flight by a series of cords. The dark air of the unfathomable sky contrasts with the tense white figures of the flyers soaring in opposite directions on wide wings of ribbed cloth.

In the *Disparate* of the woman grasped by the clothes in the teeth of a triumphant stallion he expressed in the abandoned pleasure of her smile an idea that perhaps had better have no footnotes and no gloss.

The enormous ghost shrouded and looming over the combatants of pigmy armies expresses: What price glory? It is one of the most unforgetable of his prints—this side the inscrutable *Colosso*.

[1] *The Proverbs of Goya.* By Blamire Young. Jonathan Cape. 1923.

IX
Exile
[1824–1828]

IX

Exile

[1824–1828]

1

WHEN the most savage of King Ferdinand's terrors began
in 1824 Goya was already marked for displeasure. The stinging satires he had drawn had shown what he thought of the
régime. The year before he had been one of those saved in
Duaso's house while the king's hangmen were hunting the
bravest and the best through the streets of Madrid. The two
liberal years were over; a terrorist reigned. And knowing
what lay ahead under Ferdinand's snarling tyranny, Goya
decided to join his friends in exile.

Goya's later portraits of Ferdinand, like those painted
when Charles IV abdicated, and he entered Madrid, momentarily, showed all his character. The whole story is
in the suspicious eyes and sneering mouth. A twisted childhood had made him a conspirator against his father and
mother; Napoleon's stratagem had made him a fawning
coward; the repudiation of his promises to the patriots at
Cadiz made him a traitor; he was ripe to be a tyrant. And
the most charitable historians agree that for all his pretended
interest in the arts he was the worst king Spain ever had. He
lived in nightmares, forever in fear of his life and so killing
all who might be against him. The very leader of the last
invading army that came to fight his own people and restore

him to the throne once more in 1823—the Duke of Angoulême—was sickened by Ferdinand's bloody excesses of revenge; he refused the decorations Ferdinand offered him.

Goya seldom went near Ferdinand's court. Wives died frequently in that lethal sovereign's arms; he had four of them, forever hoping for the boy heir that would have prevented the Carlist wars. It is significant that Goya painted none of Ferdinand's last three wives.

2

IT WAS not a flight. Yet it may have been a banishment. Goya had been seriously ill in 1819, when he had painted the haunting *Oración del Huerto*. The somber etchings of the *Disparate* series, we saw, a commentary on the dark state of Spain, belong also to that time. He had been some time in getting over it. And he had been sufficiently impressed with the adventure to paint, that year, the astonishing picture of himself looking suitably in extremis, with the anxious Doctor Arrieta bending over his shoulder; a kind of pieta for Æsculapius.

Now, in the early spring of 1824, he got a leave of absence to go to Plombières, in France. The ostensible object of his leaving the country was to take the mineral waters in Plombières for his health. Yet only a man in the best of health could at his age hope to stand the journey over the blistering plains of Castile and through the north and past the Pyrenees. Goya was equal to it. At seventy-eight he was once more vigorously full of life; he intended to live and paint as Titian had, till he was ninety-nine.

He was a royal painter. The leave was granted for six

months. The inescapable conclusion is that Ferdinand chose this way of removing the thorn. For among the murderous exceptions the king was making to the amnesty he had promised at Cadiz Goya would certainly be found among those who had "published anything against the state or religion"; he was not a writer, but his ideas could be more memorably expressed. Ferdinand had the satires of the *Caprichos,* the innumerable drawings lampooning both, and various paintings, to bear witness to that. Under Ferdinand the Inquisition found work to do.

Goya rode northward through the valleys where the poplars are silver against the red rock, through Alcalá where Cervantes was born, through country he had known all his life and into a land he had never seen before. Toward the end of June, Moratín wrote from Bordeaux: "Goya has actually arrived, old and deaf and not strong; he does not know a word of French, and he has no servant with him, though no one needs one more. However, he is very pleased, and very anxious to see the world." He stayed in Bordeaux three days, dining at the school Moratín, the exiled poet, was running, and talking to other exiles he had known in Madrid. He could not bring them good news from Spain, but he could tell them what was going on under Ferdinand.

He was not ready to stay in Bordeaux, far less to go and drink mineral water at Plombières. He was still "anxious to see the world," and he went on to Paris, arriving there a week before Bastille Day. Moratín, very solicitous about him, and probably laughed at for his pains, begged him to return to Bordeaux before September. He was afraid the Parisian winter would kill him. He need not have worried so. Goya apparently had no intention of doing anything except precisely what he wanted.

One wonders whether Goya saw Godoy in Paris. Carlos and Maria Luisa died in 1819. Godoy went to Paris, where, Sencourt writes, "King Louis, in view of his Bourbon marriage, made him a small allowance. He took a flat on the second floor of 20 Rue Michaudiere, and there he lived for over thirty years, tended by two women servants. His great amusement was to sit on a bench in the gardens of the Palais Royal. And there the children of the poor would ask M. Manuel to umpire their games, not knowing that he who watched them had given absolute decisions for the administration of one of the widest empires that history has seen, that he was Grand Admiral of the Fleet which had engaged with Nelson at Trafalgar, and treated, as the head of a great power, with the invincible Emperor of the French. They did not know that the mild old man who lived two floors up in the mean street close by had lived supreme among the oldest names of Spain, that he had been, like Wellington, Señor del Soto de Roma and Knight of the Golden Fleece, that the Queen of Portugal had made him Count of Evoramonte, and the Sovereigns of Spain Duke of Alcudia, Prince of the Peace, and Universal Minister of Spain and the Indies. The ring which still glittered on his finger had been placed there by a Bourbon princess, whose father was a descendant of the Grande Monarque himself.

"When he died in 1852—to be buried in Père Lachaise—Wellington too was dead, and as for Fernando VII, his bones had been resting for nearly twenty years in a sarcophagus of porphyry, while year by year at the stately altar overhead monks sang their solemn office for his soul."[1]

Goya painted two portraits of the Ferrers in Paris, and made some sketches. What he thought of the French painters of the day—Ingres, Delacroix, Gericault, Gros—we do not know, or whether he even went to the Salon. More characteristically, he made some magnificent bullfight sketches from memory before he turned southward again.

3

AND before the end of September he was back in Bordeaux. Moratín, whose letters about those days are better reading now than his poetry, said that the ineffable Leocadia Weiss was with him, and the young Rosario was there too. They had good lodgings, but apparently the ménage was not entirely serene. Leocadia had in her a touch of the shrew; Goya was not inclined to be amenable in the face of her temperament. For some time Goya was restive; though many of his old friends were around him he still wanted to travel.

His leave had been extended in January; another half year was granted him so that he could "take the waters of Bagnères." Yet he was not satisfied. In Bordeaux, as Beruete pointed out, he had around him Silvela, Goicoechea, Muguiro and the artist Brugada; they could talk endlessly about the old days. That was not enough. "At times," Moratín wrote, "he gets it into his head that he has a great deal to do in Madrid, and if he were permitted he would set out on a mule, with his cloak, his walnut stirrups his saddle bags and his *bota*"—the leather wine bottle that Spaniards use with such precision, holding it at arms length and squirting the wine down their throats.

[1]Sencourt. *Op. cit.*

The girl, Rosario, was the apple of Goya's eye; he thought she had it in her to become a great artist, though nothing she ever drew went far beyond the bounds of earnest mediocrity. There were still those who thought she was Goya's child, a calumny that is at the same time a rather admiring tribute. But he spent infinite pains over her education in art, neglecting his own drawing to teach her.

Yet he was painting a good deal, and, as Moratín said, "for dear life, without ever correcting a single line he paints." Some of his portraits of his friends and fellow exiles are among the most powerful he ever did, painted in a swift, expressive style with thick pigment, that was to be taken up in France later on. He continued with lithography, a new art then, yet one in which no master has surpassed him, as the *Toros de Burdeos* show. It was then he told Moratín he had been a bullfighter in his youth, and that with the sword in hand he feared nothing. Sketches of the street life interested him, he drew the fakers and mountebanks of a carnival, he painted miniatures. There was still an enormous amount of life in him. He enjoyed Bordeaux. One can see why, if one goes to that gray-green and pleasant town now, where good wine is cheaper than vichy water. But of Goya not much more than a plaque on the building in the Cours de l'Intendance with a ferocious profile by Benlliure that replaced the old one, now inside, remains. In the Chartreuse there is a terrible monument like a colossal British mailbox. The last place he lived in is now partly dedicated to the *majas* of Bordeaux. After changing around several times he found what he wanted, with a garden and a good light. But still he wanted to see Madrid again.

4

"Only the will remains," Goya wrote Ferrer, "for I have nothing else." But it was enough. At eighty he crossed the Pyrenees again, alone, and went back to Madrid. No one in Bordeaux could stop him. He was determined to go and he went. "If he does not arrive," Moratín said lugubriously, "do not be surprised, because the slightest accident may leave him stiff and dead in the corner of some country posada." He might have spared himself the qualm. Goya arrived triumphantly. His son was there, and Goya's restless energy, his desire to see everything that he had been thinking about in Bordeaux the past two years in exile, was boundless.

He went across the Manzanares to his old house to look at his own favorite paintings, the sardonic murals he had painted on those walls in the darkest days of his life.

Lopez, an old friend and an artist of unremarkable talent, painted Goya's portrait while he was there. He sits back proudly, the eyes heavy-lidded but still bright, the head massive, and all, somehow, reminding many who have seen it of Beethoven, with whom he had more in common than genius. Stories have gathered around that portrait. Goya is supposed to have jumped up from time to time during the sitting to demonstrate with the brush he holds various sword-plays in the bullfights they were recalling. And he is supposed to have stopped Lopez before that earnest artist was ready to call the portrait finished, so that he would not spoil it. The belief that Goya took up the palette to paint Lopez in return, and that he could not because his hands were too stiff is absurd; he was still to paint several incomparable portraits on his return to Bordeaux.

Before he was ready to return for that final exile Goya went to see his murals in San Antonio de la Florida. In the bright light around the dome he could still see old friends.

5

STILL full of life in his eightieth year, he returned to exile to die. Why did he go back to Bordeaux? Why did he not want to remain in Spain? It may be that the climate of Madrid was in its violent way of swinging from one extreme to the other not good for him. But there were other parts of Spain that would have been better. Málaga or Valencia, San Sebastian or Santander.

It is obvious, then, that he went back to Bordeaux because he wanted to leave Spain. One can see why. Ferdinand's Spain would certainly not be appealing to him. Goya, who had known the benevolent despotism of Carlos III, the fiestas and the bankruptcies of Carlos IV, the Maximilianistic efforts of Joseph Bonaparte to do good at the bayonet points of his brother's soldiers, and some years of the rule of Ferdinand, would want no more of the Spain of the year 1826.

By summer he was back in Bordeaux.

"Goya is quite well," Moratín wrote; "he amuses himself with his sketches, walks about, and sleeps during the siesta; it seems to me there is now peace in his home." The peace would be the peace of reconciliation after absence between Goya and Leocadia.

He would put the stone up and use it as though it were a drawing board. There are only four lithographs in the *Toros de Burdeos*. They give the spirit and the terrible emotion of that barbarous and ceremonious sport more than the precise details of the ring. The bulls and the men are real. The crowds are ghostly, and the ring is of unearthly proportions. Dreaming of bullfights he had seen long ago, so the drama of the bullring seemed to Goya when he was far from the land where he had taken his part in the afternoons of death.

There is no development to be traced in Goya's lithography because, as Mayer has finely said, "the earliest of his works are masterly achievements." And if it is remarkable that Goya took up lithography very late in life and "achieved things unsurpassed to this day," we must remember that he could not have taken it up much earlier, because lithography was not invented by Sennenfelder until the end of the eighteenth century, and it was some time after that before the process reached Spain.

He was still painting portraits. A year after his return to Bordeaux he signed his simple and forceful Muguiro, "by his friend Goya, painted at the age of 81 years, in Bordeaux" —he called it Burdeos, as a Spaniard—"May of 1827." Juan de Muguiro e Iribarren was a banker from Navarre, Beruete tells us, who was in exile in Bordeaux because of his liberal ideas. He was a great friend of Goya and of Goicoechea— Goicoechea was the man who was to be closest to Goya through eternity, in the Capricho of the bones.

The portrait shows Muguiro seated beside a desk, reading a letter-envelope. It is painted in the short-brushed, vibrating technique that was to make Goya the precursor of Impressionism. It is his last great portrait. He also did the Milkmaid of Bordeaux, a magnificent wench, filled with animal life and beauty. His final portrait is the unfinished Pio de Molina.

He also did two religious paintings, the Dominican and the Monk, which, as Sanchez Canton points out, prophesy Cézanne's technique.

Goya also did, as we noted, a collection of drawings of side-show freaks in Bordeaux, drawings he made at some wandering carnival. It has been suggested he meant to see if he could sell these. Many of them are signed. In them nature seems to be imitating the strange, supernal beasts of the *Caprichos*.

By now he was drawing with the help of a magnifying glass. It has been erroneously supposed that he also painted through the glass. This is absurd. He did, as his son said later, use the palette knife or the handle end of a spoon in putting on the color. As his followers were to do in the nineteenth century creation of modern painting.

One thing he may have done was that strange, un-Goya-like drawing of the two elephants with the trainer between them. It is done in a very classical, restrained way. Personally, I wonder if Goya did draw it; my heretical suspicion is that it was done by Leocadia. For it is a line drawing, and in looking at the way Leocadia was taught he specifically denounced the drawing-master style of line drawing. All he saw in nature was shades and lights, masses, planes that advance and planes that recede, he said.

Death was not far away. He had made that famous etching about death the cadaver of a man rising from the grave to trace the single, *Nada*—Nothing—on a tablet while a devouring apprehensive group looked on to learn what of eternity. He was approaching that test. And he was still feeling full of the exuberance of living.

GOYA — SELF PORTRAIT IN 1815

From the Desastres de la Guerra NO SE PUEDE MIRAR

From the Desastres de la Guerra NADA

6

BEHIND him lay more than eighty years of life. Fuendetodos with its stone-bare streets, Zaragoza, dominated by the
Inquisition and the legend of Pilar. Madrid, the wildest and
the dirtiest capital of its time in Europe. Rome, where he
had gone to find the ways of art. The court of the Bourbons.
Six years of war and ten of oppression. The painter of kings
and the scourge of follies, one of the great artists of all time
was to die in a tall house on a narrow street in Bordeaux.
The Pyrenees separated him from Spain. But Spain was in
all he drew or etched or painted.

In March, 1828, he wrote to his son, Javier, who was then
in Madrid, suggesting he send his wife and Mariano, Goya's
grandson, to Bordeaux for a visit with him. He suggested
Xavier—or Javier, he called him—come, as well. He spoke
of how they could save money there, and of the money he
had for Mariano deposited with Galos, the banker Goya had
drawn.

That was on the 12th. On the 26th he wrote:

"Dear Javier: I am very impatient, awaiting my beloved
travellers with care: of all you tell me in your last letter that
they will be with me longer on their way to Paris I am
delighted. Here they may stay with the greatest pleasure, and
if you come in the fall it will give me great joy.

"Saturday I was at the house of Galos, the banker, and
received the two drafts you sent me. I have the other letter of
979 francs, and if you send me the other two I think I'll put
them in the renta toward the 12 thousand reals a year that is
the inheritance for Mariano in perpetuity, and his descendants, isn't that so?

"I am feeling much better, and I have hopes of staying healthier than I was before the illness." He told Javier that it was Molina who had told him how to get well, by urging him to drink Baleriana, or valerian, the herb with pink or white flowers that has always been used as a mild stimulant. And: "I am very content with my improvement to receive my beloved travellers."

They arrived on the twenty-eighth of March. Goya, overjoyed at seeing them, rushed around delightedly, burned up his energy, and was furious when the tension laid him low. He added this postscript to a letter his grandson Mariano wrote Javier:

"I need not tell you more than that I was so full of joy that I felt a little indisposed, so I am in bed. God grant that you will arrive, that my joy may be complete. Adios."

The last days went swiftly. Leocadia wrote Moratín that on the first of April the family had breakfast together. But the food, spiced and Spanish, was not agreeing with Goya. On the second, desperately ill, he awoke at five in the morning.

He was unable to speak. For an hour that lasted, then, gradually, the power of speech came back to him. His side was paralyzed. In that condition he remained for thirteen days. He could recognize every one around him. Up to three hours before his death he was conscious. He told them all he wanted to make a will. Javier's wife told him he had already made it. He gradually could speak no more, looking at them all, trying to talk to them. At two in the morning, on the sixteenth of April, 1828, Francisco José Goya y Lucientes died of the apoplexy on whose margin he had lived all his furious life.

X
The Skull of Goya

X

The Skull of Goya

THE SKULL of Goya is lost. On some fantastic midnight it was stolen from the grave in Bordeaux by the gruesome followers of one or another master of phrenology whose ghoul-ridden rites flourished in those years. What a *Capricho* Goya would have made of that scene!

Goya was buried in the pleasant town of his exile. It was a pleasant town. But it was exile. And he would not gladly lie so far from Spain. There was a funeral service in the Church of Notre Dame in Bordeaux, and men of the faith whose venalities he had caricatured, and whose glories he had painted, prayed for his soul. The old friends who had shared his exile were pallbearers. He was buried in the leafy cemetery of the Chartreuse, the Order whose walls he had frescoed in another country, in the days of his young manhood at Zaragoza.

Goya had not meant to die away from Spain. There was no burial plot for him in Bordeaux. He was buried in the tomb of his friend Goicoechea, and there, under a plaque that had errors in age and date of birth and a handsome railing, he was left for more than seventy years. But he was not undisturbed. Once in the course of the years while plans official and unofficial to return his bones to Spain were being made and unmade and forgotten and remembered again, the grave robbers came and got the skull of Goya. It must have taken uncommon courage as well as uncommon ghoulishness to do that.

Where is the skull of Goya? There have been many rumors, many conjectures. Gomez de la Serna has discussed the possibility that the followers of Gall or Spurzheim had it, or that it was taken by some youth of the romantic movement. He recalled that a dozen years ago a painting appeared in Zaragoza. It was supposed to have been signed by Dionisio Fierros in 1849, and to bear on the back this inscription in the handwriting of the Marques de San Adrian: "Skull of Goya, painted by Fierros." And yet that seems only to confuse the mystery.

How could we know that Fierro had seen the skull of Goya? Once it was known that the skull had been taken from the tomb in Bordeaux the painting could easily be made. Who knew about it? Where was the painting between 1849 and 1928? Where is it now?

His demons had followed him. When the tomb of Goicoechea was opened in 1888 to take the bones of Goya back to Spain time had completed the Caprichoesque confusion. No man could say which bones in the tomb were Goicoechea's, which were Goya's. And so, with considerable pomp and circumstance, all the bones were disinterred and taken to Madrid, to lie in the imposing tomb at San Isidro, the long exile over.

It was Goya's San Isidro on the far bank of the Manzanares, where as a young man he had painted the gaieties of the fiestas and near where, in the last years before he went into exile, he had painted the somber magnificent scenes of the *Pinturas Negras*. Yet even that was not the final resting place for Goya.

And at last he was moved again. This time it was to the most appropriate place of all, to the Church of San Antonio de la Florida that in the high noon of Charles IV's flagrant reign he had painted. San Antonio de la Florida was given back to Goya, and for the parishioners a duplicate church was built a few yards away facing the river. One for God. One for Goya.

There, under the dome he painted in gold and blue and brown and scarlet, with saints that were sinners and sinners he had known and loved, he was buried for the last time.

All artists create a world for themselves. Goya created for himself an afterworld too, a mundane and glowing heaven in paint over his own resting place, a heaven of the *majos* and the *majas* of Madrid.

The skull of Goya is lost—but we have the world that was in the skull of Goya.

Appendix

Appendix

APPENDIX A

To publish a catalogue of Goya's paintings now would be to perpetuate the obsolete. When the war is over, when Spain is again at peace, it will be possible to list his paintings and drawings and their whereabouts. And it may be that then we shall have the most complete Goya catalogue of all, for it will include paintings that have been kept in hiding for many years. That catalogue will also, one hopes, exclude a few paintings and drawings now ascribed to Goya with a generosity toward the ability of whatever anonymous hand actually painted them that has always seemed excessive.

Meantime, the best catalogues available are those in Mayer, Beruete, Loga, Delteil, Stokes and Calvert. They are all out of date now, all inaccurate in parts. But they present an enormously valuable collection of material about the works of Goya.

APPENDIX B

The Caprichos

The *Caprichos* are still Goya's most widely known series of etchings. They need no explanation—yet as long as they exist there will be interest in the interpretation of them. There are many "keys," and most of them are obvious—even the interesting one supposedly by Goya. The following list of the plates, together with explanations from various sources—notably the works of Beruete, Mayer, Calvert, Achiardi, Viñaza and the so-called "Ms. Ayala"—was compiled as a supplement to the text. Goya's commentary is from Mayer, largely as translated by Robert West; the other interpretations, and the mistakes, are my own.

1. *Goya, Pintor*

Portrait of the artist, jaw thrust out, wearing the tall hat that accentuates his serene truculence. One of the best of all the self-portraits. This was not originally intended for the frontispiece, which was to have been the plate of "El sueño de la razón produce monstruos."

2. *El sí pronuncian y la mano alargan al primero que llega*
(They say yes—and give their hands to the first man who presents himself.)

A young girl, masked, being led to the altar by an elderly horror. Based on a play by Moratín.
Goya's (supposed) commentary: "The frivolity with which many women enter matrimony in the hope of being able to gain greater liberty by it."

3. *Que viene el coco*

(Here comes the bogey man.)

Children flying to their mother from a hooded apparition.
Goya's commentary (again, *supposed*, as it has never been proved that he wrote the comments ascribed to him as they are quoted throughout this appendix): "Injurious misuse of early education. To bring a child to fear the bogey man more than his father and so make it afraid of something that does not exist."

[248]

4. *El de la Rollona*

(The Grown-up Child.)

A lackey with a man dressed as a child in leading strings. Believed, Calvert observes, to symbolize the helplessness and dependence of the rich on their servants.

Goya's commentary: "Carelessness, undue want of strictness, and spoiling makes children capricious, naughty, vain, greedy, lazy and insufferable. They grow up and yet remain childish. That is the big spoilt child."

5. *Tal para qual*

(You can translate this as Greek meets Greek or Birds of a Feather or any number of similar maxims.)

A *maja* and a *majo*.

Goya: "It is often disputed whether man or woman is worse by nature but the vices of the one and the other come from bad up-bringing. Where the men are perverted, the women are the same. The young lady portrayed in this etching is as good as the young fop talking to her, and as regards the two old people one is as vile as the other."

Ms. Ayala: "Maria Luisa and Godoy."

6. *Nadie se conoce*

(No one knows himself.)

Masked persons in conversation. Again Calvert: "Supposed to suggest that in this world we know each other only by appearances."

Goya: "The world is a masquerade. Face, dress and voice, all are false. All try to seem what they are not, all deceive and do not even know themselves."

7. *Ni así la distingue*

(Even so he cannot recognize her.)

Another gallant eying a lady through a glass.

Goya: "Why should he recognize her? No spectacles are strong enough; one would need judgment and knowledge of the world and both these things the poor gentleman has not got."

8. *Que se la llevaron!*

(And so she was carried off.)

A woman being kidnapped.

Goya's commentary: "The woman who cannot take care of herself belongs to the first man who seizes her, and yet, when it is too late, people are surprised that she has been carried off."

9. *Tántalo*

(Tantalus.)

The man in despair over a woman who is dead or overcome.

Goya: "If he were more gallant and less of a bore she would come to life again."

10. *El amor y la muerte*

(Liebestod, or Love and death)

A woman holding in her arms a man who has just been mortally wounded in a duel.

Goya: "See here a Calderonian lover, who, unable to triumph over his rival, dies in the arms of the woman he loves, losing her by his daring. It is a pity to draw the sword too often."

11. *Muchachos al avío*

(Boys, be up and doing!)

Four brigands—Andalusian, Calvert thinks—under a tree.

Not a characteristic one to spring to mind when you think of the *Caprichos*.

Goya: "Their faces and clothes show what they are."

APPENDIX

12. *A caza de dientes*

(Hunting for teeth.)

This is the famous *Capricho* of the woman pulling a tooth from a hanged man. It seems to me Goya had, perhaps, a specific instance in mind. It's as topical as the drawing of the women with the quicklime, though it expresses a popular superstition.

Goya's commentary: "The teeth of a man who has been hanged are very efficacious for sorceries; without this ingredient nothing succeeds. What a pity that people should believe such nonsense!"

13. *Están calientes.*

(They are hot.)

The *Capricho* shows friars at dinner. Goya says: "They are hot." Yet don't take the picture too literally in considering what Goya meant to say.

Goya: "They are so greedy that they swallow their soup too hot. Even in pleasure temperance and discretion are necessary."

14. *Qué sacrificio!*

(What a sacrifice!)

The young girl and the repellent bridegroom. An idea Goya used satirically over and over again. Once in a tapestry, once in a painting that's at the Museo Romantico, called *La Segunda Boda del Joro-bado*—the hunchback's second marriage.

Goya: "It is true that the bridegroom is not very pleasant to look at, but he is rich, and at the cost of the liberty of one poor child the maintenance of a hungry family is bought. It is the way of the world."

[251]

APPENDIX

15. *Bellos consejos*

(Counsels of beauty—Good advice.)

The old woman telling the young girl what a beauty needs to know.

Goya: "The advice is worthy of her who is taking it. The worst of it is that the girl will follow it to the letter. Unhappy the man who has anything to do with her!"

According to theories sometimes held, this represents Godoy's famous and ultimately—when he was in exile—faithless mistress, Tudo.

16. *Dios la perdone: y era su madre*

(God forgive her—it was her mother.)

Goya's commentary: "The girl left her home in early youth. She spent the time of her apprenticeship at Cadiz, then went to Madrid. There she won the first prize. She goes for a walk in the Prado and hears a dirty, shrivelled hag begging her for alms; she sends her away, the old hag follows her. The hard-hearted girl turns round and finds—who would think it possible—that the poor old woman is her mother!"

17. *Bien tirada está*

(She's well dressed.)

The girl drawing up her stocking. This must be the *Capricho* Baudelaire remembered.

Goya: "Oh, 'Tia Cura' is no fool! She knows quite well that stockings must fit tight around the leg."

18. *Y se le quema la casa*

(And his house is burned down.)

A drunkard undressing, unaware he's set the house on fire.
Goya: "He couldn't take off his breeches properly, nor could he

[252]

stop playing about with the candle till the fire engines of the town revived him. That is what wine can do."

19. *Todos caerán*

(They'll all fall.)

Men being plucked.

Goya: "Those who are to fall are never warned by the example of those who have fallen before them. It is no use, they will fall, every one."

20. *Ya van desplumados*

(They're plucked.)

The girls chasing the plucked man-headed birds. Those heads must be portraits. Whose?

Goya: "When they have no more feathers send them off! Others will come along."

21. *Qual la descanonan!*

(How they pluck her!)

Cat-headed lawyers pluck a bird with a woman's head.

Goya: "Hens are plucked by vultures. As the saying is: 'Give and take.' 'Six of one and a half a dozen of the other.'"

Ms. Ayala: "Skit on the judges, who take sides with officers of the law so as to be able to plunder the harlots with impunity."

22. *Pobrecitas!*

(Poor little fools.)

Two girls accosted by two officers. I have not ever been sure whether Goya said it in plain satire or double-satire. "Poor little things!"

Goya: "They will have to mend what is torn asunder, to repair what has long been allowed to go from bad to worse."

Ms. Ayala: "Poor harlots are sent to prison—rich ones go free."

23. *Aquellos polbos*
(Those ashes.)

A dunce-capped woman hearing her sentence at the hands of the Inquisition.

Goya: "For shame! to treat her in this fashion, an honorable woman who has waited on every one for a trifle, so industrious, so useful."

24. *No hubo remedio*
(There was no remedy.)

Calvert: "A woman, stripped to the waist and mounted on an ass, is led away by the officers of the Inquisition."

Goya: "They are determined to kill this saintly woman. After judgment had been pronounced against her (*despues de escribirla la vida*) she is dragged through the streets in triumph. She has indeed deserved a triumph, but if they do it to shame her they are wasting time. No one can make her ashamed who has nothing to be ashamed of."

25. *Si quebró el cántaro*
(The jar was broken.)

Mother spanking boy for breaking the smashed jar in the background.

Goya: "The boy is a scamp and the mother bad-tempered. A pretty pair!"

Ms. Ayala: "Maria Luisa and the Crown Prince Ferdinand."

26. *Ya tienen asiento*
(They've got seats now.)

Women—barelegged and bare-thighed—wearing chair seats down on their heads. That's where their seats are, it seems to me Goya suggests, if their brains are.

Goya: "These good girls have seats enough and nothing to do with them better than to put them on their heads."

APPENDIX

27. *Quien más rendido?*

(Which the more devoted?)

Who's the more bored? The fop or the courtesan he's charming?
Goya: "Neither cares for the other. He is a charlatan in love who says the same things to every woman he meets, and she is wondering how to fit in five assignations between 8 o'clock and 9—and it's half-past seven now!"
Ms. Ayala: "Goya and the Duchess of Alba." Compare Goya's comment!

28. *Chitón*

(Shh!)

A *maja* of fashion summons an old beldam. The Spanish custom of having beggars deliver love letters.
Goya: "An excellent mother to trust with an important message."

29. *Esto sí que leer*

(He calls this reading.)

A man reading languidly while his hair is being dressed.
Goya: "He is having his hair combed and his stockings drawn on and sleeps and studies the while. No one can say he is not making the most of his time."
Ms. Ayala: "The King's ministers fail to inform themselves of the state of affairs till the very last moment."
Mayer takes this to be a woman.

30. *Por qué esconderlos?*

(Why hide them?)

It's plain Goya meant the man trying to hide his moneybags from four hooting bystanders as a monk or a priest.

Goya: "The answer is easy. He won't spend it and doesn't spend it because although he is over 80 and has barely another month to live he is afraid that he might live longer and have no more money left. So mistaken are the calculations of avarice!"

31. *Ruega por ella*

(She prays for her.)

An old woman praying while a girl's dressing to go out on the town.

Goya: "And she did well to do so—that God might send her luck and keep her from harm and from leeches and bailiffs and make her as dextrous and wily and wide awake and ready as her sainted mother."

32. *Por qué fué sensible*

(Because she was sensitive.)

A girl weeping in jail.

Goya: "As was to be expected! The world has its ups and downs. The life she led could end in no other way."

33. *Al Conde Palatino*

(To the Count Palatine.)

The famous *Capricho* of the men spewing while a charlatan pulls teeth. "Allusion, probably, to the practice of such gentry of representing themselves as physicians to foreign potentates."—Calvert.

Goya: "In all sciences there are quacks who know everything without having learned, and have a remedy for everything. One can't believe what they say. The really educated person always mistrusts their too great conclusiveness and plausibility, and himself makes moderate promises and keeps much in reserve. But the Count Palatine fulfills none of his promises at all."

APPENDIX

34. *Las rinde el sueño*

(Sleep overcomes them.)

Sleep gives them solace. Women asleep in prison. Women of the town.

Goya: "Don't wake them! Sleep is the only happiness of the unfortunate."

35. *Le descañona*

(She shaves him.)

The young girls shave the young man.

Goya: "They strip him of all he has. It is his own fault for putting himself in such hands."

36. *Mala noche*

(A bad night.)

Woman and the night they're out in both bad.

Goya: "To such dangers are the street walkers exposed, who won't stay home."

This one has been supposed to be aimed at Maria Luisa.

37. *Si sabrá mas el discípulo?*

(What if the pupil knows more?)

A donkey pompously teaches a smaller ass.

Goya: "It's difficult to say, but certainly the teacher is very much in earnest."

This one has been called a "skit on the shallow lessons in politics given to Godoy by Acuna and Mollinedo.")

38. *Brabísimo!*

(Wonderful!)

A donkey applauds a monkey who plays on a guitar. I think there's little question that Godoy and the King—who fancied himself as a musician—are intended here.

Goya: "If the size of the ears make a good listener he should be a most informed person. But it is to be feared that he is applauding ignorantly."

39. *Asta su abuelo*

(As far as his grandfather.)

A donkey looking over a page of portraits of other donkeys. They're his ancestors. It's not only a satire on the follies of pedigree. It's a furious thrust at such ways of establishing "racial purity."

Goya: "The poor wretch has been driven mad by genealogists and heralds. He isn't the only one."

40. *De que mal morirá?*

(Of what ill will he die?)

A donkey doctor feeling a very sick man's pulse.
Goya: "The doctor is doing his best—what more can he want?"
This has been supposed to refer to Goya's doctor.

41. *Ni más ni menos*

(An exact likeness! Neither more nor less.)

Calvert: "A donkey sits for his portrait to a monkey, who is painting a horse. Satire on artists who paint pictures of those whom they have never seen." But why of those whom they have never seen? What of those artists—and Goya, it seems to me meant them—who paint people as better than they are, for flattery and profit? As for it's being a monkey who's painting, there's the familiar expression, pintamonas—painting monkey.

Goya: "It is fortunate that he had his portrait painted. Now those who do not know him will (who have not seen him will) know what he is like."

Mayer, page 81: "(Antonio Carnicero painting Godoy's portrait.)" Carnicero's picture here alluded to was not produced until several years after the *Caprichos!* The Ms. Ayala calls it "Doctor Golilla having his portrait painted."

42. *Tú que no puedes*

(Thou who canst not.)

Calvert: "Two men staggering under the weight of two asses. The men represent the people, the asses perhaps the governing classes."

(From the refrain of the song: "Thou who canst not carry me on thy shoulder.")

Goya: "You can't deny that these two cavaliers are cavalry (*que estos dos caballeros son caballerías*) riding horses."

Mayer, p. 81: " 'The working classes bear the whole social burden; they are regular beasts of burden.' Satire upon taxation? (The secretaries Urquijo and Caballero—who, by the way, were friends of Goya—are supposed to have been attacked here, but they came into office after the *Caprichos* were published!)"

43. *El sueño de la razón produce monstruos*

(The dream of reason produces monsters.)

It is with this etching—the artist, head on arms at his drawing table, fantasms behind him and around his head—that the *Caprichos* change, from the natural to the intimations of the supernatural. (Except such as 54, 55, 72, 73, 75.)

Goya: "Imagination deserted by reason begets impossible monsters. United with reason she is the mother of all art and the source of its wonders."

This was the original title page of the *Caprichos*. It was inscribed: "Ydioma universal. Dibujado y grabado pr Fco Goya año 1797." But Mayer (91) points out that it "was not intended for the original title-page but was produced as the last of the 'original Caprichos' as proved by the date, 1797, on the preliminary drawing." Yes, but it might still have been intended, at one point, for the title page, and it seems to me it's hard to interpret the inscription "Ydioma universal" any other way.

44. *Hilan delgado*

(Finely do they spin.)

The old witches spinning.
Goya: "Finely do they spin, and the devil himself will not be able to tear what they are weaving."

45. *Mucho hay que chupar*

(There is plenty to suck.)

Three witches taking snuff around a basket full of new-born infants.
Goya: "Those who reach the age of eighty suck little children dry, those who do not live beyond eighteen suck big children. It seems that man is born in this world and lives, simply to have the marrow sucked out of him."
Mayer recalls that Lefort thought this meant Godoy.

46. *Corrección*

(Correct guidance.)

A Congress of Sorcerers.
Goya: "Without correction and punishment one cannot get on in

any science and in that of witchcraft one needs uncommon talent, industry, mature age and strict obedience to the teachings of the Great Witchmaster, who conducts the seminary of Barahona."

Ms. Ayala: "The tribunal of the Inquisition."

47. *Obsequio a el Maestro*

(Homage to the maestro.)

Hag-witches offer a newborn child to their master.

Goya: "That is only right; they would be ungrateful scholars indeed not to entertain their professor, to whom they owe all their knowledge of the diabolic science."

48. *Soplones*

(Bellows blowers. Also slang for spies, stool pigeons.)

A bat-winged witch at work.

Goya: "The 'blowing witches' are the most disgusting of all the devil's league and the most stupid. If they had any sense they would not try to blow."

Mayer says this is an "alleged satire on auricular confession."

49. *Duendecitos*

(Little goblins.)

Dwarf-goblins at their play.

Goya: "Quite a different kind of little people! Jolly, quick, helpful; a little greedy, a little prone to play naughty tricks, but very nice, good-natured fellows."

50. *Los chinchillas*

(The chinchilla rats.)

Calvert: "Two persons with costumes heraldically decorated, their eyes closed, and with padlocks on their ears, are being fed by a third, blindfolded and with ass's ears. Allusion to the aristocracy, represented to be the victims of superstition and ignorance."

Goya: "People who neither hear nor know, nor do anything, belong to the numerous family of the Chinchilla rats and were never yet good for anything."

51. *Se repulen*

(They pare.)

Demons engaged in clipping each other's nails.

Goya: "To have long nails is so nasty and slovenly that it is forbidden even in the society of witches."

52. *Lo que puede un sastre!*

(What a tailor can do!)

Calvert: " 'What a tailor can do!' Devotees prostrate themselves before an ecclesiastical vestment hung on a tree."

Goya: "Very often some silly fellow, a mere nonentity, is got up to look like some one of importance. This effect is produced by the tailor's art and the stupidity of people who only judge by outward appearance."

53. *Que pico de oro!*

(What a beak of gold!)

A parrot preaching to the cloth.

Goya: "This looks like an academic session. Perhaps the parrot is speaking on medical science? However, don't believe what he says. There is many a doctor who has a 'golden beak' when he is talking but is useless when it comes to writing prescriptions. He can discuss diseases in the most able manner, but he can't cure them. He makes fools of sick people and fills the church yards with skulls."

54. *El vergonzoso*

(The disgraceful one.)

The disgraceful one—eating from a dish held by another.

Goya: "There are many people whose faces are the most shameless things in their whole bodies and it would be a good thing if those who have such unfortunate and ridiculous countenances were to hide them in their breeches."

Mayer points out this "rightly belongs to the first series."

55. *Hasta la muerte*

(Till death.)

A hag—looking singularly like the Queen—trying on a headdress before a mirror while bystanders look on derisively.

Goya: "She is quite right to smarten herself up. It is her birthday. She will be seventy-five and her female friends are coming to see her."

Ms. Ayala: "The old Duchess of Osuna."

Mayer points out this is another that "rightly belongs to the first series."

56. *Subir y bajar*

(Ups and downs.)

A satyr holds one figure aloft while others crash and are crushed. Rise and fall—of Godoy? (Ms. Ayala.)

Goya: "Fortune is unkind to those who court her. Efforts to rise are rewarded by emptiness and those who have risen she punishes by downfalls."

57. *La filiacion*

(The stud book.)

An animal-masked group gathering, discussing ancestry.

Goya: "Here they are fooling the bridegroom by showing him

the patent of nobility, who the parents, grandparents, great-grand-parents and great-great grandparents of the young lady were. But who is *she?* He will find that out later."

58. *Trágala, perro*

(Swallow it, dog!)

As Calvert sees it: "A monk threatens with an enormous syringe a kneeling priest surrounded by other monks." The syringe may be filled with quicklime as in the drawing in the Madrazo album of Fortuny's at the Metropolitan.

Goya: "Who ever lives among people will surely be subjected to annoyances. If he wants to avoid them he must live in the wilderness but even there he will soon discover that loneliness is also an annoyance."

59. *Y aun no se van!*

(They haven't gone yet!)

And still they don't go. Two blasted ancients staggeringly hold up a looming slab. The desperate clinging to life.

Goya: "He who does not reflect on the inconstancy of fortune sleeps calmly though surrounded by dangers. Nevertheless he cannot avoid the danger which threatens him and there is no misfortune which may not befall him."

Mayer recalls that Lefort suggested this meant the royal family.

60. *Ensayos!*

(First attempts.)

Trials. Look at it: The man learning sorcery from the naked woman, the great goat in the background.

Goya: "Gradually he makes progress. He can already jump a little and in time he will know as much as his teacher."

APPENDIX

61. *Volaverunt*

(They have flown.)

A *maja*—drawn as Goya always drew the Duchess of Alba—soars through the air with one foot on the triangulated crouched backs of three figures—toreros, perhaps.

Goya: "The group of witches which serves as pedestal to this fashion's fool is ornamental rather than useful. There are heads so swelled with gas that they need neither balloon nor witches to make them fly."

Ms. Ayala: "The Duchess of Alba standing on the heads of three toreros."

And I have wondered whether no sacrilege (or parody of Murillo) was intended.

62. *Quien lo creyera!*

(Who would have thought it?)

Two stripped figures fight furiously as they fall to the death symbolized by monsters reaching to receive them.

Goya: "Here is a bitter quarrel about which of the two is the greater witch. Who would have thought that these two would tear each other to pieces in such a fashion? Friendship is a daughter of Virtue. Rogues may be accomplices, but not friends."

Mayer, 82 (Ms. Ayala?): "Of these two riders on a monster, half bear and half donkey, one is *Tappu*, but an impostor, the other is as brutal as he is generous. Such are kings and their ministers among the nations, yet the people call for them when they are absent and desire to be governed by them."

63. *Miren que grabes*

(Look how solemn they are!)

Goya: "The etching shows two decent and much-respected witches out for a ride."

APPENDIX

64. *Buen viaje!*

(Bon voyage!)

A salute to the witches that soar through the darkness of Spanish sorcery.

Goya: "Where is this hellish company going, filling the air with noise in the darkness of night? If it were day time, it would be quite a different matter; the whole lot would be brought down to earth by gun shots. But as it is night no one can see them."

Compare the two flying men, in the Quinta murals.

65. *Dónde va mama?*

(Where is mother going?)

She is going into witchcraft. Three demons are carrying her off. The cat that is a Goya symbol of witchcraft holds a parasol over them, the owl that is a Goya symbol of witchcraft spreads wings under the crotch of the lowest demon.

Goya: "Mother has dropsy and has been sent out for a walk. God grant she may recover."

66. *Alla va eso*

(That's the way it goes.)

Goya: "A witch is riding on a limping devil. This poor devil at whom every one laughs is useful sometimes."

67. *Aguarda que te unten*

(Wait till you've been anointed.)

A goat—one foot human—struggles upward to be free of two demons calmly preparing to anoint him from a bowl. Calvert: "Alleged by some to be a derisive allusion to the sacrament of extreme unction."

Goya: "He has been sent out on an important errand and wants to go off half greased. Even among the witches some are thoughtless, indiscreet, imprudent, without the least judgment of their own. It is the same everywhere."

Mayer, 82: "Alleged parody on extreme unction. Viñaza thinks this explanation correct—it seems impossible to me—and to be accounted for by Goya's allegiance to Voltaire."

68. *Linda maestra!*
(Beautiful mistress!)

A witch soars on her broomstick toward the symbolic owl. Behind her a woman—not another witch, as some say—her face hidden, her hair suggesting the Duchess.

Goya: "The broom is one of the most necessary implements for a witch, for besides being useful for sweeping, as can be gathered from many tales, it can be changed into a mule which can go at such a pace that even the devil himself can't catch up with it."

69. *Sopla*
(She blows.)

She uses a swung child as a bellows. Beyond the quiet horror of the witchcraft, the figures above, a woman holding children under the wings of an unearthly figure, there is the further horror of the crouched strained clamorous figures below.

Goya: "No doubt there was a great catch of children yesterday. The banquet prepared here will be a rich one. Make a hearty meal!"

70. *Devota profesion*
(Devout profession.)

A woman with symbolic ass' ears (women do as the clergy tells them now?), seated on a centaur, reads from a book two Inquisition-capped ecclesiastics hold out to her with pincers.

Goya: " 'Will you swear to obey your masters and those set in authority over you, to honor them, to sweep the garrets, to spin oakum, to beat drums, to howl, to yell, to fly, to cook, to grease, to suck, to bake, to blow, to roast, everything and what ever time you are ordered to do so?' 'I swear.' 'Very well then, my daughter, you are a witch. Hearty congratulations.' "

Mayer, 82: "Thought by Loga to be a satire on the Holy Trinity."

71. *Si amanece, nos vamos*

(At dawn we must be off.)

In the starred darkness a demon who has been lecturing hag-witches points to the high horizon, women of households behind his back.

Goya: "If you hadn't come you wouldn't have been missed."

72. *No te escaparas*

(You shall not escape.)

A girl being told by man-faced demons: "You won't escape."
Goya: "No one ever escapes who wants to be caught."
Ms. Ayala: "Godoy as a lover pursuing the Dutén."

73. *Mejor es holgar*

(It is better to be lazy.)

A girl stands beside a man who's seated on a bag of goods, helping a beldam. She—the beldam—is greedily triumphant, he's disfigured by despair. Don't, Goya is saying, get tangled up that way. It's better to sport.

Goya: "If he who works does not enjoy it he is quite right to say: 'It is better to go easy.' "
Another of Mayer's nominations for the first series.

APPENDIX

74. *No grites, tonta*

(Don't scream, you little fool.)

Two cassocked phantoms before a delightedly frightened girl.

Goya: "Poor Panchita! She was looking for the footman and she met the goblin. But don't be afraid. The goblin is in good temper and won't do her any harm."

75. *No hay quien nos desate?*

(Will no one set us free?)

A man and a woman bound together while the bird of clericalism holds his watch over them: "Will no one set us free?"

Goya: "A man and a woman are tied together with ropes. They are trying with all their might to loosen them and calling for some one to come and set them free. If I am not much mistaken they are two people who have been forced to marry."

Mayer would put this in the first series, in spite of the fantastic owl.

76. *Esta V^{md} ... ? Pues, como digo: ... eh! Cuidado si no ...*

(Are you listening? Well, as I say ... eh ... Look out! If not ...)

A foolish, fat and foppish officer chuffing with portentous, wander-witted orders, while those who face him look sadly bored, those who are behind him jeer.

Power tends to brutalize.

Goya: "The cockade of rank and the baton of command make this blockhead imagine himself to be a superior being. He misuses the office of commander entrusted to him to annoy every one who knows him. He is proud, vain, insolent to all who are below him, cringing to all more powerful than he."

APPENDIX

77. *Unos a otros*

(One to another.)

Calvert: "Old dotards attacking a third who is playing at 'ball.' May be intended to convey a satire on the aged who pretend to the activities and energy of youth."

Calvert means bull for ball. One wears the wicker-and-horns children in Spain put over their heads to play bullfighting. The two old fool nobles are mounted on servant's backs, they tilt with lanzas like picadors.

Goya: "It is the way of the world. People laugh at each other and play bullfighting with one another. He who yesterday played the part of the bull today plays the torero. Fate presides over the show and provides the allotment of parts according to her caprice."

78. *Despacha, que despiertan*

(Quick, they're waking up.)

Calvert: "An old woman apparently awaking her fellow servants." I doubt that. They're all witches, they've been raising hob with the house while the people slept, it's time to leave.

Goya: "The elves are most industrious and helpful little people. As the maid is friendly with them they clean the pot, cook the vegetables, dust and sweep and look after the baby. People argue about their being devils or not. That is quite a mistake. Devils are those who are busy making mischief or hindering others from doing good or doing nothing whatever."

79. *Nadie nos ha visto*

(No one has seen us.)

Monks carousing with flagons beside a keg in a cellar.
Goya: "And what does it matter if the elves do go down into the

wine cellar and have a glass of wine after they have worked all night and the bung shines like bright gold?"

80. *Ya es hora*

(It's time.)

Monk-demons stretching and getting ready to go out. They wear miniature human skeletons where a bunch of keys would hang.

Goya: "When the dawn comes they fly away, each to his place, witches, hobgoblins, dreams and phantoms. It is as well that these creatures only show themselves by night and that no one has found where they hide by day. But if anyone raided a goblin den and were to show them in a cage at ten in the morning in the Puerta del Sol it would be worth a fortune to him."

These three belong with the *Caprichos:*

81. The dream of lies and inconstancy.

82. The lamenting women, with the man giving a dog medicine.

83. The girl sleeping in prison, her feet chained and manacled.

Acknowledgments

In the course of two journeys to Spain before the war began I received generous help toward the understanding of Goya and the material about him from many people there, especially the staffs of the Prado, the Academia de Bellas Artes de San Fernando, the Calcografía Nacional and the Biblioteca Nacional, in Madrid. To them all I should like to express my gratitude and recall the pleasure of those days.

I am also gratefully indebted to the staffs of the Hispanic Society of America, the Frick Art Reference Library, the New York Public Library and the Metropolitan Museum of Art for a great deal of assistance in avoiding many more errors than even this version of a book that has threatened pleasantly but somewhat impractically in the last four years to become a life's work still undoubtedly contains.

For the almost improbable patience and courtesy of Maxwell E. Perkins, William Weber, and other members of the Scribners staff in the face of my lamentable dilatoriness, all my thanks are rather on the inadequate side.

Finally, I am enormously indebted on many pages to the authors, living and dead, of innumerable works—monographs, histories, articles, critiques and commentaries about Goya and Goya's Spain.

Bibliography

Bibliography

ACHIARDI, Pierre d'. *Les dessins de D. Francisco Goya y Lucientes au Musée du Prado a Madrid*. 3 volumes. Rome. 1908.

AGUILERA, Emiliano M. *Las Pinturas Negras de Goya. Historia, Interpretación y Crítica*. Madrid: Ediciones Nuestra Raza. 1936.

AGUILERA, Emiliano M.–F. Carlos Sainz de Robles. *Reproducción Fotografica de los Cuadros, Cartones, Dibujos y Aguafuertes Mas Notables del Famoso Pintor Goya*. Madrid: J. G. Guiñón. 1933.

AMICIS, Edmondo de. *Spain*. Translated by Wilhelmina W. Cady. New York: G. P. Putnam's Sons. 1881.

AÑO ARTISTICO. Madrid. 1918.

ARAUJO, Sánchez Zeferino. *Goya*. Madrid: La España Moderna. 1895.

ARAUJO, Sánchez Zeferino. *La España del Siglo XIX*. Madrid.

ARTE ESPAÑOL. Madrid. Año 18, Tomo 9.

BERUETE Y MORET, Aureliano de. *Goya, Pintor de Retratos*. Madrid, 1916. *Goya, Composiciones y Figuras*. Madrid, 1917. *Goya, Grabador*. Madrid, 1918.

BERUETE Y MORET, Aureliano de. *Goya*. The three books above compiled into one volume by F. J. Sánchez Cantón. Madrid. 1928.

BERUETE Y MORET, Aureliano de. *Goya as Portrait Painter*. Translated by Selwyn Brinton. Boston: Houghton Mifflin Company. 1922.

BIBLIOTHÈQUE NATIONALE. *Goya. Exposition de l'Œuvre Gravé, de Peintures, de Tapisseries et de Cent Dix Dessins du Musée du Prado*. Paris. 1935.

BOIX, Felix–F. J. Sánchez Cantón. *Cien Dibujos Inéditos de Goya*. Madrid: Museo del Prado. 1928.

BRUUN, Geoffrey. *Europe and the French Imperium. 1799–1814*. New York: Harper & Brothers. 1938.

[277]

BIBLIOGRAPHY

BURLINGTON MONOGRAPH—II. *Spanish Art*. New York: E. Weyhe. 1927.

CALVERT, Albert F. *Goya. An Account of His Life and Works With 612 Reproductions from His Pictures, Etchings and Lithographs*. London: John Lane, The Bodley Head. 1908.

CARDERERA, Valentín–Philip Burty. *François Goya, Sa Vie, Ses Dessins et Ses Eaux Forts*. Gazette des Beaux Arts, 1860, VII, 1863, XV.

CASANOVA, Jacques. *The Memoirs of Jacques Casanova de Seingalt*. Translated by Arthur Machen. 2 volumes. New York: Albert & Charles Boni. 1932.

CATÁLAGO *Illustrado de la Exposicion de Pinturas de Goya, Celebrada Para Conmemorar el Primer Centenario de la Muerte del Artista*. Madrid: Museo del Prado. 1928.

CHAPMAN, Charles E. *A History of Spain. Founded on the "Historia de España y de la Civilizacion de España" of Rafael Altamira*. New York: The Macmillan Company. 1918.

COLECCIÓN *de Cuatrocienas Cuarenta y Nueve Reproducciones de Cuadros, Dibujos y Aguafuertes de Don Francisco de Goya. Procedidos de un Epistolario del Gran Pintor y de las "Noticias Biográficas" Publicadas por Don Francisco Zapater y Gómez en 1868*. Madrid: Editorial Saturnino Calleja. 1924.

COOPER, Duff. *Talleyrand*. New York: Harper & Brothers. 1932.

COSSÍO, Manuel B. *Enciclopedia Popular Ilustrada de Ciencias y de Artes. Pintura*. Madrid. 1885.

CRASTRE, François. *Goya*. Translated by Frederic Taber Cooper. New York: Frederick A. Stokes Company. 1912.

CRAVEN, Thomas. *Men of Art*. New York: Simon & Schuster. 1931.

CRUZADA VILLAAMIL, G. *La Casa del Sordo*. Madrid: El Arte en España. 1868.

CRUZADA VILLAAMIL, G. *Los Tapices de Goya*. Madrid. 1870.

DARD, Émile. *Napoleon and Talleyrand*. Translated by Christopher R. Turner. New York: D. Appleton-Century Company. 1937.

DELACROIX, Eugène. *The Journals of Eugène Delacroix*. Translated by Walter Pach. New York: Covici-Friede. 1937.

DELTEIL, Lois. *Le Peintre-Graveur Illustré*. Vols. XIV, XV. Paris. 1922.

BIBLIOGRAPHY

DERWENT, Lord. *Goya, an Impression of Spain.* London: Methuen & Company. 1930.

ELLIS, Havelock. *The Soul of Spain.* Boston: Houghton Mifflin Company. 1915.

ENCINA, Juan de la. *Goya en Zig Zag.* Madrid. 1928.

ERSKINE, Mrs. Steuart. *Madrid.* New York: E. P. Dutton & Co. 1923.

EZQUERRA DEL BAYO, Joaquín. *El Palacete de la Moncloa.* Madrid. 1919.

EZQUERRA DEL BAYO, Joaquín. *La Duquesa de Alba y Goya.* Madrid: Libreria de Ruiz Hermanos. 1928.

FAURE, Elie. *The Disasters of War. Eighty-Five Etchings by Goya.* With an Introduction by Elie Faure. New York: Oxford University Press. 1937.

FAURE, Elie. *History of Art.* Vol. IV: *Modern Art.* Translated by Walter Pach. New York: Harper & Brothers. 1924.

FITZMAURICE-KELLY, James. *A New History of Spanish Literature.* New York: Oxford University Press. 1926.

FLITCH, J. E. Crawford. *An Idler In Spain.* New York: McBride, Nash & Co. 1914.

FORD, Richard. *A Handbook for Travellers in Spain.* London. 1845.

GAUTHIER, Théophile. *Voyage en Espagne.* Paris. 1845.

GIVRY, Grillot de. *Witchcraft, Magic and Alchemy.* Translated by J. Courtenay Locke. Boston: Houghton Mifflin Company. 1931.

GÓMEZ DE LA SERNA, R. *Goya.* Madrid: Ediciones la Nave. 1928.

GRAPPÉ, Georges. Goya dans les Collections de France. (L'Amour de L'Art.) Paris: Éditions Hypérion. 1938.

GUEDALLA, Philip. *Wellington.* New York: Harper & Brothers. 1931.

HAGEN, Oskar Frank Leonard. *Patterns and Principles of Spanish Art.* Madison: University of Wisconsin Studies in Language and Literature. Number 38. 1936.

HAMERTON, Philip Gilbert. *Portfolio Papers.* Boston: Roberts Brothers. 1889.

HARRIS, E. *Spanish Painting.* Paris: The Hyperion Press. 1937.

HOFFMANN, J. *Francisco de Goya. Katalog seines graphischen Werkes.* Vienna. 1907.

BIBLIOGRAPHY

HOLLAND, Elizabeth. *The Spanish Journal of Elizabeth Lady Holland*. Edited by the Earl of Ilchester. New York: Longmans, Green & Co. 1910.

HUME, Martin A. S. *Modern Spain. 1788–1898*. New York: G. P. Putnam's Sons. 1900.

IVINS, William M. *A Note on Goya. (Prints and Their Makers*. Edited by Fitzroy Carrington.) New York. 1912.

LAFOND, Paul. *Les dernières années de Goya en France*. Gazette des Beaux Arts. 1907.

LAFOND, Paul. *Goya*. Paris. 1902.

LAFUENTE FERRARI, Enrique. *Las Pruebas de Estado de "Los Desastres de la Guerra" en la Biblioteca Nacional*. Madrid: Tipografia de Archivos. 1934.

LANGDON-DAVIES, John. *Behind the Spanish Barricades*. New York: Robert M. McBride & Co. 1936.

LATIMER, Elizabeth Wormesley. *Spain in the Nineteenth Century*. Chicago: A. C. McClurg & Co. 1897.

LEFORT, Paul. *Francisco Goya. Étude biographique et critique suivi de l'essai d'un catalogue raisonné de son œuvre gravé et lithographié*. Paris. 1877.

LOGA, Valerian von. *Francisco de Goya*. Berlin. 1903.

LOGA, Valerian von. *Francisco de Goya. Meister der Graphik Band IV*. Leipzig: Klinkhardt und Biermann.

LOW, D. M. *Edward Gibbon. 1737–1794*. New York: Random House. 1937.

MADARIAGA, Salvador de. *Spain*. New York: Charles Scribner's Sons. 1930.

MADOL, Hans Roger. *Godoy, the First Dictator of Modern Times*. London: Hurst & Blackett. 1934.

MADRAZO, Pedro de. *Catálago descriptivo e historico del Museo del Prado de Madrid*. Madrid. 1872.

MADRAZO, Pedro de. *Goya. Almanaque de la Ilustración Española y Americana*. Madrid. 1880.

MATHERON, Laurent. *Goya*. Paris: Schulz et Thullie. 1858.

MAYER, August L. *Francisco de Goya*. Translated by Robert West. London & Toronto: J. M. Dent & Sons, Ltd. 1924.

McMAHON, A. Philip. *Goya, the First Modern*. The Arts. Vol. 10, No. 2. 1936.

BIBLIOGRAPHY

MESONERO ROMANOS, Manuel. *Goya, Moratín, Meléndez Valdés y Donoso Cortés*. Madrid. 1900.

METROPOLITAN MUSEUM OF ART. *Francisco Goya, His Paintings, Drawings and Prints*. New York: The Metropolitan Museum of Art. 1936.

MORATÍN, Leandor F. *Obras Postumas. Tomo III. Correspondencia particular desde Burdeos*.

MUSÉE DE L'ORANGERIE. *Peintures de Goya des Collections de France*. Paris. 1938.

MUTHER, Richard. *The History of Modern Painting*. In four volumes. New York: E. P. Dutton & Co. 1907.

OERTEL, Richard. *Goya*. Leipzig: Verlag von Velhagen & Klafing. 1929.

PARIS, Pierre. *Goya*. Paris: Librairie Plon. 1928.

PEERS, E. Allison. *Spain*. New York: Dodd, Mead & Co. 1929.

PEREYRA, Carlos. *Cartas Confidenciales de la Reina Maria Luisa y de Don Manuel de Godoy. Con otras tomadas del Archivo reservado de Fernando VII, del Historico Nacional y de las Indias*. (Los Archivos Secretos de la Historia.) Madrid: M. Aguilar. 1935.

PEREZ Y GONZÁLES, Felipe. *Un Cuadro de Historia*. Madrid. 1910.

PRADO. *Museo del Prado: Catálogo*. Madrid. 1933.

REINACH, S. *Apollo, An Illustrated Manual of Art Throughout the Ages*. New York: Charles Scribner's Sons. 1904.

ROTHENSTEIN, William. *Goya*. The Artist's Library. London: at the Sign of the Unicorn. 1900.

RAZA ESPAÑOLA. Año 2. Madrid. 1920.

SAINZ DE ROBLES, F. Carlos. *Historia y Estampas de la Villa de Madrid*. Two volumes. Madrid: Iberia. 1935.

SALCEDO RUÍZ, Ángel. *La Época de Goya*. Madrid: Editorial Saturnino Calleja. 1924.

SÁNCHEZ CANTÓN, F. J. *Goya*. (Traduction Française de George Pillement.) Paris: G. Crès & Cie. 1930.

SÁNCHEZ CANTÓN, F. J. *Los Dibujos del Viaje a Sanlúcar*. Madrid. 1928.

SÁNCHEZ CANTÓN, F. J. *Sala de los Dibujos de Goya*. Madrid: The Prado. 1928.

BIBLIOGRAPHY

SÁNCHEZ DE RIVERA, Daniel. *La Enfermedad de Goya*. Madrid: Revista Española de Arte. Año IV, Numero 5. Marzo. 1935.

SEDGWICK, Henry Dwight. *Spain, a Short History*. Boston: Little, Brown & Co. 1926.

SENCOURT, Robert. *The Spanish Crown, 1808–1931*. New York: Charles Scribner's Sons. 1932.

SINGLETON, Esther. *Old World Masters in New World Collections*. New York: The Macmillan Company. 1929.

SOCIEDAD ESPAÑOLA DE EXCURSIONES. *Boletín*. Año 36, Trim. 1. Madrid. 1928.

STARKIE, Walter. *Spanish Raggle-Taggle*. New York: E. P. Dutton & Co. 1935.

STARKWEATHER, Wm. E. B. *Paintings and Drawings by Francisco Goya in the Collection of the Hispanic Society of America*. New York: 1916.

STIRLING-MAXWELL, Sir William. *Annals of the Artists of Spain*. London: 1891.

STOKES, Hugh. *Francisco Goya. A study of the Work and Personality of the Eighteenth Century Spanish Painter and Satirist*. New York: G. P. Putnam's Sons. 1914.

SWINBURNE, Henry. *Travels Through Spain in the Years 1775 and 1776*. London: Printed by J. Davis for P. Elmsly in the Strand. 1787.

TERASSE, Charles. *Goya y Lucientes, 1746–1828*. Paris: Librairie Floury. 1931.

TILD, Jean. *Goya*. Paris. 1921.

TRAPIER, Elizabeth du Gue. *Catalogue of the Paintings (Sixteenth, Seventeenth and Eighteenth Centuries) in the Collection of the Hispanic Society of America*. New York. 1929.

UNIVERSIDAD. Numero 1. Año 5. Zaragoza. 1928.

VELASCO Y AGUIRRE, Miguel. *Grabados y Litografías de Goya*. Madrid: Espasa Calpe. 1928.

VIÑAZA, Conde de la. *Goya, Su Tiempo, Su Vida, Sus Obras*. Madrid. 1887.

VIÑAZA, Conde de la. *Adiciones al Diccionario de Cean Bermudez*. Madrid. 1894.

WEHLE, Harry B. *An Album of Goya's Drawings*. Bulletin of the

BIBLIOGRAPHY

Metropolitan Museum of Art, Volume XXXI. New York: 1936.

WEHLE, Harry B. *Fifty Drawings by Francisco Goya.* New York: *Papers* of the Metropolitan Museum of Art. Number 7. 1938.

YOUNG, Blamire. *The Proverbs of Goya. Being an Account of "Los Proverbios," Examined and Now for the First Time Explained.* London: Jonathan Cape. 1933.

YRIARTE, Charles Emile. *Goya, sa biographie, les fresques, les toiles, les tapisseries, les eaux-fortes, et la catalogue de l'œuvre.* Paris: Henri Plon. 1867.

ZAPATER Y GÓMEZ, Francisco. *Apuntes históricos biográficos acerca de la Escuela Aragonesa de Pintura.* Madrid. 1863.

ZAPATER Y GÓMEZ, Francisco. *Goya, Noticias Biográficas.* Zaragoza: La Perserverencia. 1868.

ZIGROSSER, Carl. *Six Centuries of Fine Prints.* New York: Covici-Friede. 1937.

Index

Index

INDEX

INDEX

INDEX